Ace Aca
ACHIEVING EXCE

MW00451364

THE ONE BIG BOOK

GRADE 1

For English, Math, and Science

★ Includes Math, English, Science - all in one colorful book

★ Detailed instructions to teach and learn with pictures and examples

★ Best book for home schooling, practicing, and teaching

★ Includes answers with detailed explanations

Detailed instructions along with interesting activities

www.aceacademicpublishing.com

Author: Ace Academic Publishing

Prepaze is a sister company of Ace Academic Publishing. Intrigued by the unending possibilities of the internet and its role in education, Prepaze was created to spread the knowledge and learning across all corners of the world through an online platform. We equip ourselves with state-of-the-art technologies so that knowledge reaches the students through the quickest and the most effective channels.

The materials for our books are written by award winning teachers with several years of teaching experience. All our books are aligned with the state standards and are widely used by many schools throughout the country.

For enquiries and bulk order, contact us at the following address:

3736, Fallon Road, #403
Dublin, CA 94568
www.aceacademicpublishing.com

Ace Academic Publishing
ACHIEVING EXCELLENCE TOGETHER

This book contains copyright material. The purchase of this material entitles the buyer to use this material for personal and classroom use only. Reproducing the content for commercial use is strictly prohibited. Contact us to learn about options to use it for an entire school district or other commercial use.

ISBN: 978-1-949383-35-5
© Ace Academic Publishing, 2019

Other books from Ace Academic Publishing

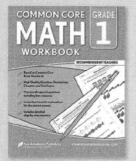 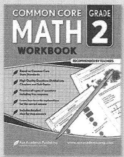 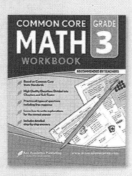 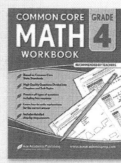 

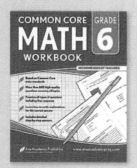 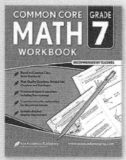 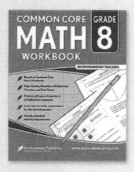  

Ace Academic Publishing

ACHIEVING EXCELLENCE TOGETHER

Other books from Ace Academic Publishing

Ace Academic Publishing
ACHIEVING EXCELLENCE TOGETHER

Contents

English

Math

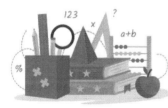

Science

English

This book enables your children to explore the English language and develop the necessary expertise. A series of thought-provoking exercises, engaging activities, and engrossing puzzles facilitate your children with understanding the intricacies of the English language.

Uppercase and Lowercase Letters

In English alphabet, each letter can be written as an uppercase (capital) letter or a lowercase (small) letter.

Aa Bb Cc Dd Ee Ff Gg
Hh Ii Jj Kk Ll Mm Nn
Oo Pp Qq Rr Ss Tt Uu
Vv Ww Xx Yy Zz

Connect the Pictures

Do you know your letters? Draw lines to connect the letters with the pictures that begin with these letters. Not all the letters may have a matching picture.

Using the dotted lines, trace the letters A to Z.

Aa Bb Cc Dd Ee

Ff Gg Hh Ii Jj

Kk Ll Mm Nn Oo

Pp Qq Rr Ss Tt

Uu Vv Ww Xx Yy

Zz

Pair It Up!

Match the lowercase and uppercase letters with objects starting with the same letter.

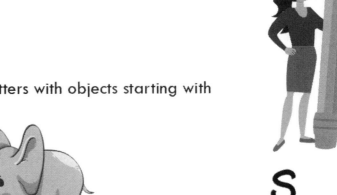

l		S
c		P
P		E
e		C
s		L

Circle the matching lowercase letters.

1	S	k	n	s	i
2	D	b	d	m	o
3	Q	q	b	a	z
4	K	v	n	e	k
5	G	r	t	x	g
6	E	c	e	a	j
7	R	h	r	b	p
8	C	l	n	c	s
9	Y	e	k	o	y
10	H	i	h	z	f

prepaze

1. j   s   D   b   n

2. Q   c   E   M   Y

3. i   N   O   U   F

4. h   s   z   d   X

5. P   A   k   v   o

6. W   C   L   Z   e

7. d   x   B   v   r

8. R   a   D   G   K

Fill in the blanks with the uppercase letters.

1. f   ___ A N

2. m   ___ A T

3. b   ___ I K E

4. r   ___ O S E

5. p   ___ E N

6. s   ___ E E

7. v   ___ A N

8. j   ___ A M

What Am I?

Write the names of the pictures below in lowercase (small) letters.

1

2

3

4

5

6

7

8

prepaze

Mirror image of a word differs from the actual word. However, there are a few words that look the same in the mirror.

Write these words on a notebook and see their reflection in a mirror.

TOOT	
YAY	
OTTO	

Can you think of more such words? Use a mirror to check your work.

Nouns

Nouns are naming words for people, places, and things. There are different types of nouns. Below are examples of three types of nouns.

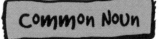

This is a **car**.

Sam plays football.

This is my **friend's** book.

Complete Me!

Fill in the blanks with the words given in the box.

cat	children's	balloon	Tina's	Mike

1. Erin is _____ sister.

2. Did you see my _____ ?

3. This is a _____ playground.

4. Lisa and _____ are planting trees.

5. I want a _____ .

Common Noun

A common noun is a common name used to refer to a person, place, or thing.

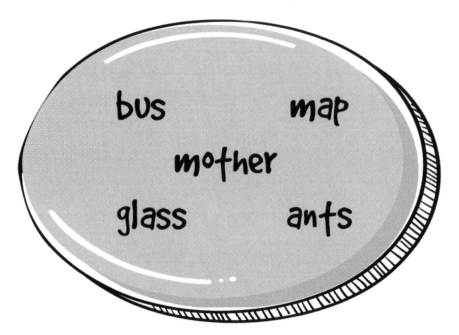

Find Me!

Underline the common nouns in the below sentences.

1. It is a board.

2. The basket has oranges and grapes.

3. Ana's friend has a garden.

4. This lake is amazing!

5. Joe is in the house.

Proper Noun

A proper noun is a specific name used to refer to a person, place, or thing. It is written with a capital letter.

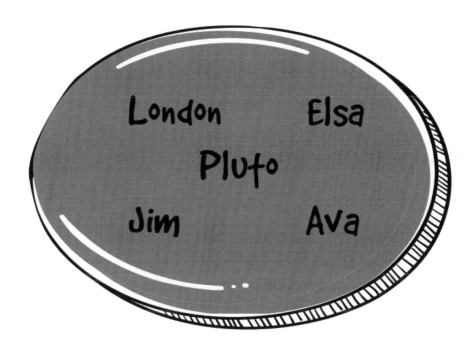

Underline the proper nouns in the below sentences.

1. I can read English.

2. Pluto is not a planet.

3. His name is John.

4. Lisa and Mike watered the trees.

5. Joe is writing.

prepaze

A possessive noun is used to show ownership or possession.

shirt's collar

phone's case

parent's house

Underline the possessive nouns in the below sentences.

1. Is this my friend's bike?

2. She is going to her brother's school.

3. I painted the dog's house.

4. The wall's color is yellow.

5. It is Lily's.

Miss Jones   Chair   book   Sam's bag

window   table   Andy   wall

Categorize the words in the box into the correct basket.

Ava's dog	tennis	Mia's pen	Tom
doctor	Jim	desk	fish
Tim's kite	Sun	garden	Adam

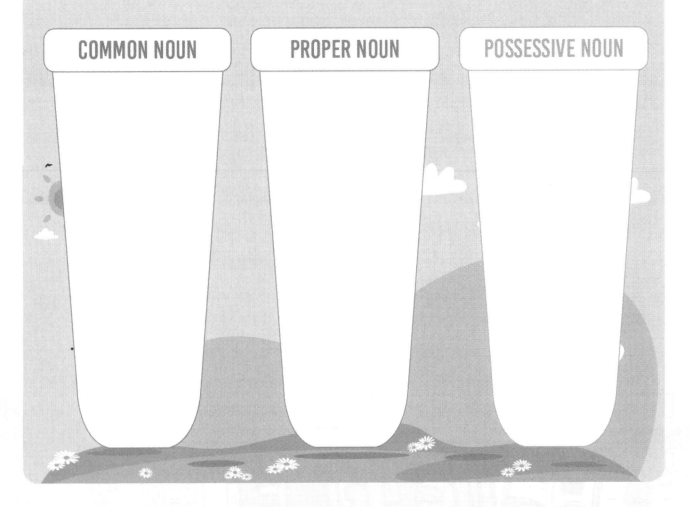

COMMON NOUN

PROPER NOUN

POSSESSIVE NOUN

Color Me

Find the type of noun underlined in the sentence and color the correct option.

1. We chased the <u>birds</u>.

| Common Noun |
| Proper Noun |
| Possessive Noun |

2. <u>Darla's</u> jokes are funny.

| Common Noun |
| Proper Noun |
| Possessive Noun |

3. <u>Vince</u> is happy.

| Common Noun |
| Proper Noun |
| Possessive Noun |

4. The <u>beach</u> is beautiful.

| Common Noun |
| Proper Noun |
| Possessive Noun |

5. <u>Jane</u> takes the bus.

| Common Noun |
| Proper Noun |
| Possessive Noun |

Secret Word

Find the secret word by naming each animal.

Draw 4 nouns and color them. Label each drawing.

Nouns and Matching Verbs

In a sentence, a subject and a verb should agree in number. A singular noun needs a singular verb. A plural noun needs a plural verb.

Examples

Singular	Singular
David 	David **plays** in the park.
Plural The boys 	**Plural** The boys **play** in the park.

What's My Plural?

Write the plural form of the singular verbs.

1.  follows

2.  wears

3.  barks

4.  rides

5.  plants

6.  brings

Pair It Up!

Match the subject on the left with the predicate on the right.

The cat	sail in the sea.
Children	runs fast.
Adam	growls.
Cows	hop along the wall.
Ships	graze in the meadow.

This or That?

1. The baby _____ (sleep, sleeps).

2. The students _____ (learn, learns).

3. The teacher _____ (read, reads) the book.

4. Jerry _____ (comb, combs) his hair every day.

5. The girls _____ (swim, swims) in the pool.

Combine and Use

Form sentences using the nouns and verbs from the given boxes.

Nouns	Your Sentence	Verbs
The boys		(sing, sings)
The dog		(dig, digs)
The girl		(dance, dances)
Animals		(is, are)
The desk		(is, are)

prepaze

Pick out the singular verbs

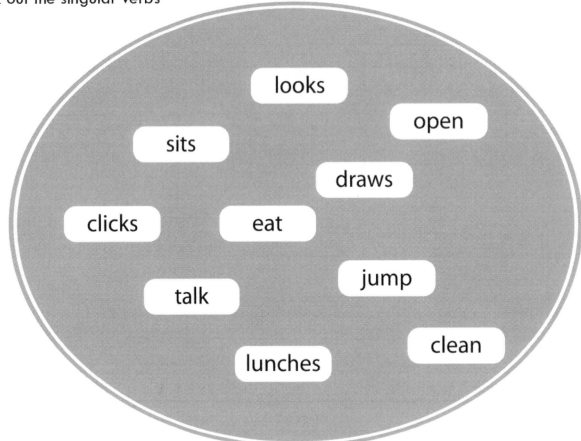

looks

open

sits

draws

clicks   eat

jump

talk

clean

lunches

1. _____

2. _____

3. _____

4. _____

5. _____

Circle the sentence in which the nouns and the verbs agree in number.

1. The car is on the road.   The car are on the road.

2. My brothers laughs.   My brothers laugh.

3. Tom lives in this street.   Tom live in this street.

4. They clean the house.   They cleans the house.

5. My friend visits the doctor.   My friend visit the doctor.

6. The cats run.   The cats runs.

Write sentences using the pictures.

1.

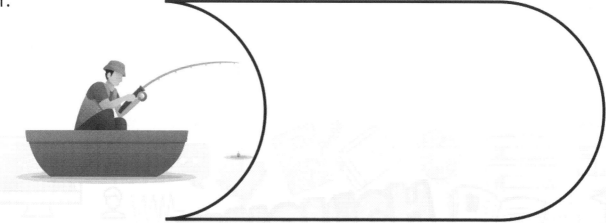

2.

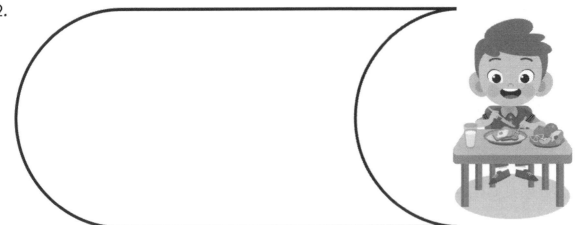

3.

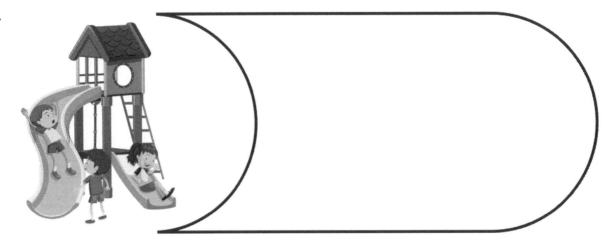

4.

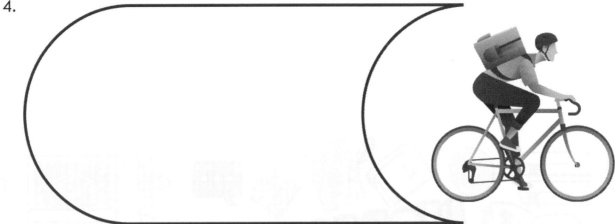

5.

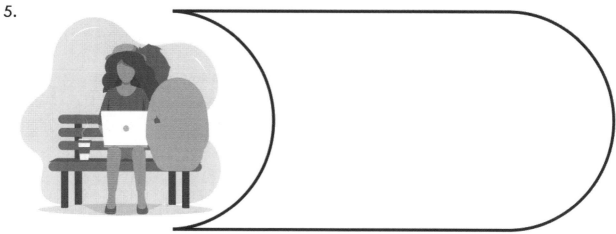

Connect the dots to reveal the hidden creature. Color it and have fun.

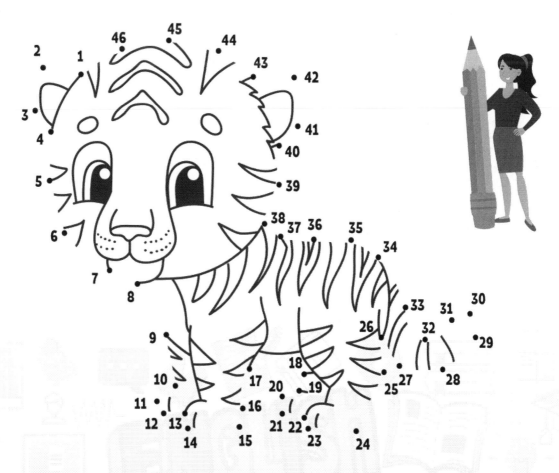

Prepositions

Prepositions link a noun or pronoun to other words in a sentence.

Examples

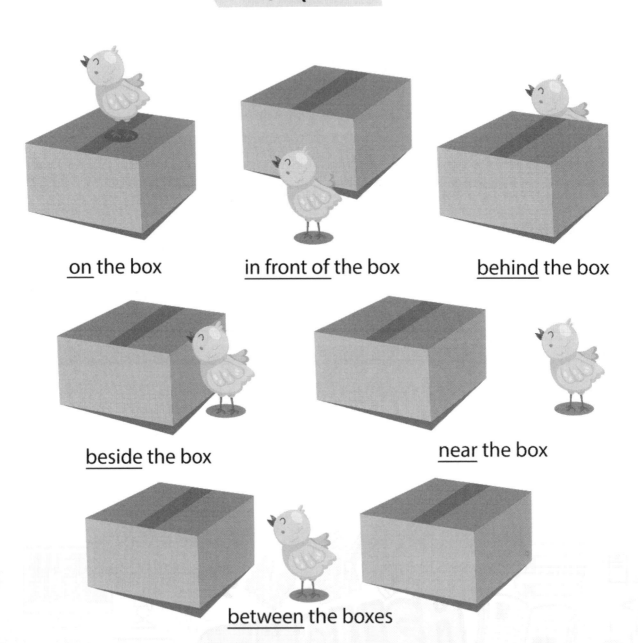

on the box

in front of the box

behind the box

beside the box

near the box

between the boxes

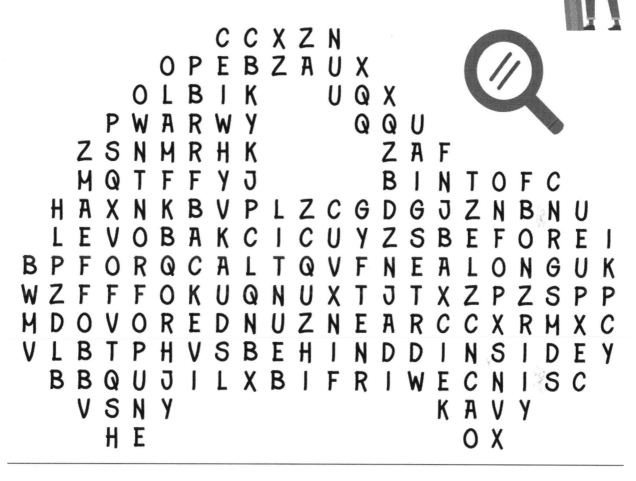

```
          C C X Z N
        O P E B Z A U X
        O L B I K     U Q X
      P W A R W Y     Q Q U
    Z S N M R H K       Z A F
    M Q T F F Y J       B I N T O F C
  H A X N K B V P L Z C G D G J Z N B N U
  L E V O B A K C I C U Y Z S B E F O R E I
B P F O R Q C A L T Q V F N E A L O N G U K
W Z F F F O K U Q N U X T J T X Z P Z S P P
M D O V O R E D N U Z N E A R C C X R M X C
V L B T P H V S B E H I N D D I N S I D E Y
B B Q U J I L X B I F R I W E C N I S C
  V S N Y                   K A V Y
    H E                       O X
```

ABOVE	UNTIL	BEFORE
BEHIND	FRONT	OFF
FOR	BACK	UNDER
INTO	SINCE	ALONG
NEAR	INSIDE	

Locate the cat

Show where the cat is in each of these pictures using prepositions.

prepaze

Circle the prepositions

1. They   sell   toys   in   their   shop.

2. We   use   umbrellas   during   rain.

3. She   is   walking   toward   the   hospital.

4. The   worm   went   behind   the   vase.

5. I   feel   something   inside   my   bag.

6. The   floor   feels   cold   under   my   feet.

7. We   went   with   our   parents.

8. We   can   see   beyond   this   river.

Fill in the blanks using the given words

under	around	by	during	in

1. The cat is sitting _____ the table.

2. We use umbrella _____  rain.

3. The hyenas are _____ the tree.

4. The animals are _____  the zoo.

5. The mermaid swam _____ the boat.

Sentence Writing

Write sentences using 4 of these prepositions.

across	after	at	from	up	with

01

02

03

04

Did You Know?

Adding an "s" to a noun makes it plural, whereas adding an "s" to a verb makes it singular.

Singular Noun

friend

Plural Noun

friends

Singular Verb

sings

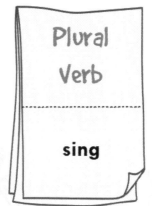

Plural Verb

sing

Pronouns

Pronouns

Pronouns are words that replace a noun
(name of a person, place, or thing) in a sentence.

Personal Pronouns

Personal pronouns are used to replace the name of a person.
(Examples: I, he, you, me, she, they, us)

I like deer.
She likes deer.

Circle the correct personal pronouns:

1. _____ love my mother.

a. He

b. You

c. I

prepaze

2. _____ is my elder brother.

a. She

b. He

c. They

3. _____ is playing with her friend Susan.

a. They

b. She

c. You

4. Both of _____ are on the same team.

a. them

b. we

c. I

5. _____ both went to a movie.

a. We

b. She

c. He

Possessive Pronouns

Possessive pronouns are used to show possession.
(Examples: his, hers, yours, mine)

> These fruits are **mine**.
>
> It's **yours**.

Circle the correct possessive pronouns:

1. This is Annie, and this is _____ book.

a. its

b. her

c. his

2. This is my dog, and _____ collar is new.

a. yours

b. mine

c. its

3. Sam and July called _____ parents.

a. their

b. his

c. her

4. This is my sister, and this is _____ house.

a. its

b. your

c. our

5. David is my friend, and I like _____ cat.

a. his

b. their

c. mine

Indefinite Pronouns

Indefinite pronouns are words that do not refer to a particular person, place, or thing. (Examples: some, any, all, one, everybody, many)

We finally moved to **another** house.

You **all** are invited.

Circle the correct indefinite pronouns:

1. _____ took my pencil.

a. Someone

b. Anything

c. Somewhere

2. We can go _____ by train.

a. nothing

b. anywhere

c. somebody

3. _____ is possible if you try hard.

a. Anywhere

b. Anything

c. Someone

4. _____ people like basketball.

a. Many

b. Something

c. Nothing

5. _____ on the team supports the coach.

a. Anywhere

b. Nowhere

c. Everyone

prepaze

you	my	our	everyone	us

Did _____ see _____ robot?

Hi _____!

Do you want to play with _____ toys?

Hello Patrick! Come and join _____.

Match and Color

Shade the matching personal and possessive pronouns with the same color.

1. it   yours

2. we   mine

3. he   theirs

4. you   its

5. I   ours

6. they   his

Pair It Up!

For every sentence on the left with a personal pronoun, there is a matching sentence on the right with a possessive pronoun. Connect the matching pairs.

Personal Pronoun	Possessive Pronoun

1. I played with my football.　○　○　a. The car is ours.

2. She had your apples.　○　○　b. This mobile phone is hers.

3. We have a car.　○　○　c. The football I played with was mine.

4. This is her mobile phone.　○　○　d. Is this bag yours?

5. Is this your bag?　○　○　e. The apples she had were yours.

Sorting Game

Categorize the pronouns.

I	hers	someone	his	ours	anywhere
mine	you	we	he	everyone	yours
she	nobody	something	them	each	

Personal Pronoun	Possessive Pronoun	Indefinite Pronoun

Tenses

Verbs are words that indicate action or state of being.

There are three forms of verb tenses:

Past Tense	Present Tense	Future Tense
Donald **played** football yesterday.	Tim **plays** baseball.	Cathy **will play** tennis tomorrow.

Describe the Picture

Write 4 sentences using the picture. One is done for you.

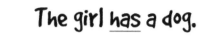

The girl has a dog.

Sentence 1

Sentence 2

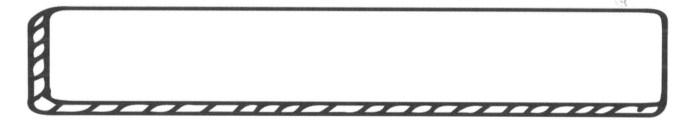

Sentence 3

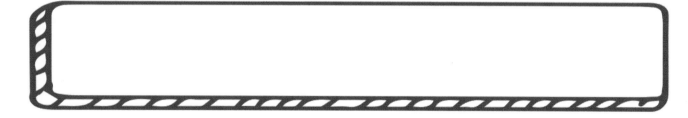

Sentence 4

prepaze

Present Tense

It refers to an action or state that generally or currently exists.

Examples

The sun **rises** in the east.

He **is** late.

This or That?

Choose the correct present tense verb.

1. Jack _____ to school regularly. (goes, will go)

2. Rene _____ in the park daily. (walks, walked)

3. Kim _____ on the phone for long. (talks, will talk)

4. Smith _____ on his bed often. (jumps, jumped)

5. Maxim always _____ the heavy boxes. (lifts, lifted)

Past Tense

It refers to an action or state that has happened.

Examples

The boy called.

The dog was happy.

Choose the correct past tense verb.

1. My mom _____ me with my homework last night. (helps, helped)

2. Oliver _____ the work an hour ago. (finishes, finished)

3. Nancy _____ me for dinner. (invites, invited)

4. Dane _____ his tutor for help. (asks, asked)

5. Larry _____ an apple in the morning. (eat, ate)

Future Tense

It refers to an action that has not yet happened.

Examples

The girl **will call**.

The cat **will stay** here.

This or That?

Choose the correct future tense verb.

1. They _____ at 12:30pm today. (arrive, will arrive)

2. I _____ you later. (see, will see)

3. Louis _____ early tonight. (sleeps, will sleep)

4. Julie _____ tomorrow. (comes, will come)

5. Hold on! Grace _____ in a few minutes. (reaches, will reach)

conjugate

Write the past tense of the given verb using -ed

1. walk _____

2. jump _____

3. play _____

4. work _____

5. push _____

6. knock _____

7. boil _____

8. cook _____

9. talk _____

10. pull _____

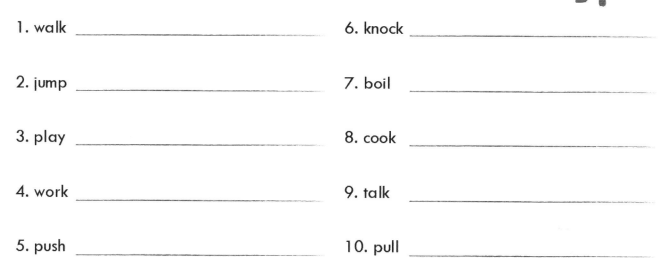

Write the future tense of the given verb by adding "will"

1. eat _____

2. say _____

3. wash _____

4. learn _____

5. sing _____

6. do _____

7. bring _____

8. stand _____

9. learn _____

10. run _____

Write the present tense verb.

1. will go _____

2. cleaned _____

3. tried _____

4. rang _____

5. will know _____

6. cut _____

7. said _____

8. will fetch _____

9. rode _____

10. will give _____

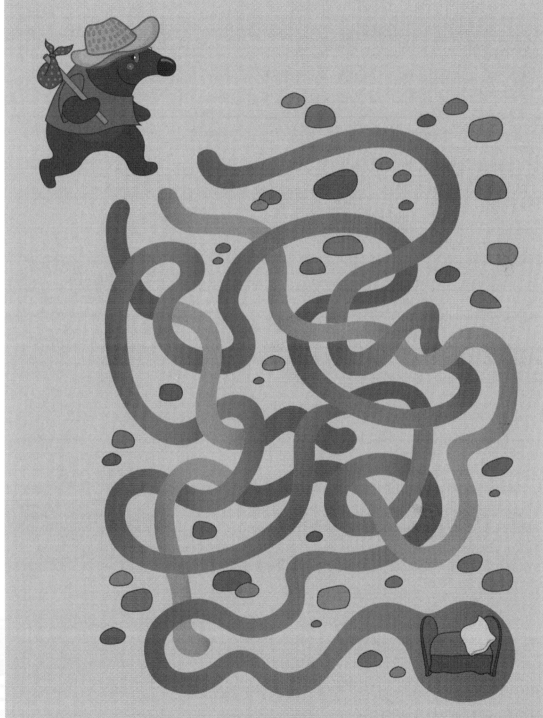

Adjectives

Adjectives are describing words in a sentence. They modify a noun (a person, animal, place, or thing). They can go before or after the words they modify.

Examples

round table

gray butterfly

big truck

The words round, gray, and big are words that give more information about the given objects.

Guess the Mood

Connect the adjectives with the pictures.

1. happy

2. angry

3. shocked

4. sad

5. sleepy

Spot the Adjectives

Circle the words that are adjectives.

car   coat   tall

huge   red   hard

soft   Mary   father

good   cat   little

books   first   poor

Adjectives

Complete the below sentences with appropriate adjectives.

| endless | worried | scared | loyal | messy |

1. Our dog is _____ of the fireworks.

2. My room is never  as I clean it often.

3. The _____ guard helped us.

4. We shop at the mall where the choices are _____.

5. When we reach home late, our mom gets _____.

Describe Me

Add an adjective for each noun.

1. | _____ | ghost

2. | _____ | leaves

3. [_____] crab

4. [_____] book

5. [_____] star

This or That?

Choose the correct adjective.

1. Vance has an _____ bicycle. (old, three)

2. Mark opened his_____ bag. (bad, new)

3. The _____ fox ran. (bright, old)

4. The bus has _____ wheels. (four, soft)

5. She likes _____ leaves. (colorful, third)

Coloring Fun

Color the picture. Then add an adjective for each word taken from the picture.

_____ bird

_____ leaves

_____ bear 1

_____ bear 2

_____ sky

_____ tree

Frequently Used Conjunctions

Conjunctions are words used to connect words or parts of a sentence.

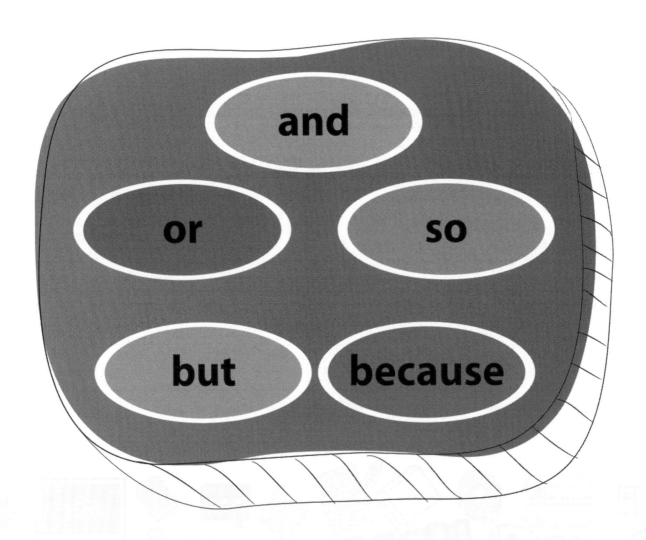

Crossword Puzzle

Complete the crossword puzzle using the clues.

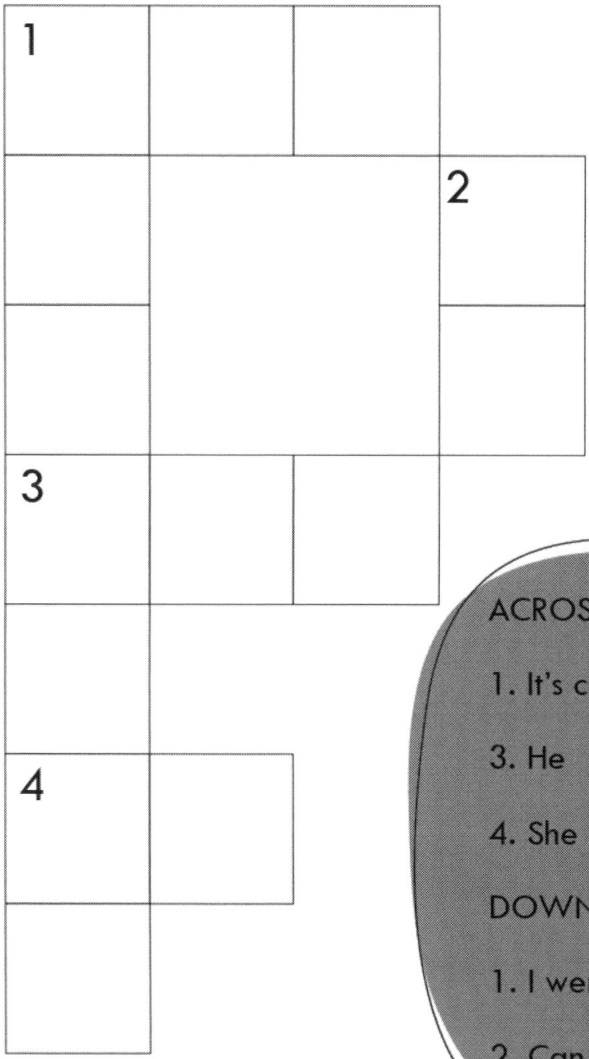

ACROSS

1. It's challenging, ... we can try.

3. He .... I are there.

4. She is kind, ... she helps.

DOWN

1. I went .... I wanted to.

2. Can you find a pen .... pencil?

Circle the conjunctions.

1.   John   and   Alfred   are   captains.

2.   You   can   color   the   chilly   red   or   green.

3.   I   am   excited   because   tomorrow   is   New   Year.

4.   David   missed   it   because   he   came   late.

5.   Mary   is   watching   Tom   and   Jerry.

6.   Steve   likes   to   pitch,   but   he   does   not   like   to   bat.

7.   Susie   and   I   have   the   same   dress!

8.   The   clothes   were   dirty,   so   I   washed   them.

9.   Do   you   want   to   get   your   red   or   green   hat?

10.   I   was   hungry,   so   I   had   an   apple   juice.

 YES or No

Does the sentence have a conjunction? Color the YES or NO box accordingly.

S.No	Sentences	YES	No
1	My name is Joe.		
2	Ann and Gina are friends.		
3	Excuse me. May I use your phone?		
4	The bus was late because of rain.		
5	My opinion differs from yours.		
6	Wood floats, but iron sinks.		
7	Kelly opened the door.		
8	I can't hear anything because of the noise.		
9	Jeff may or may not win.		
10	Rabbit eats carrots.		

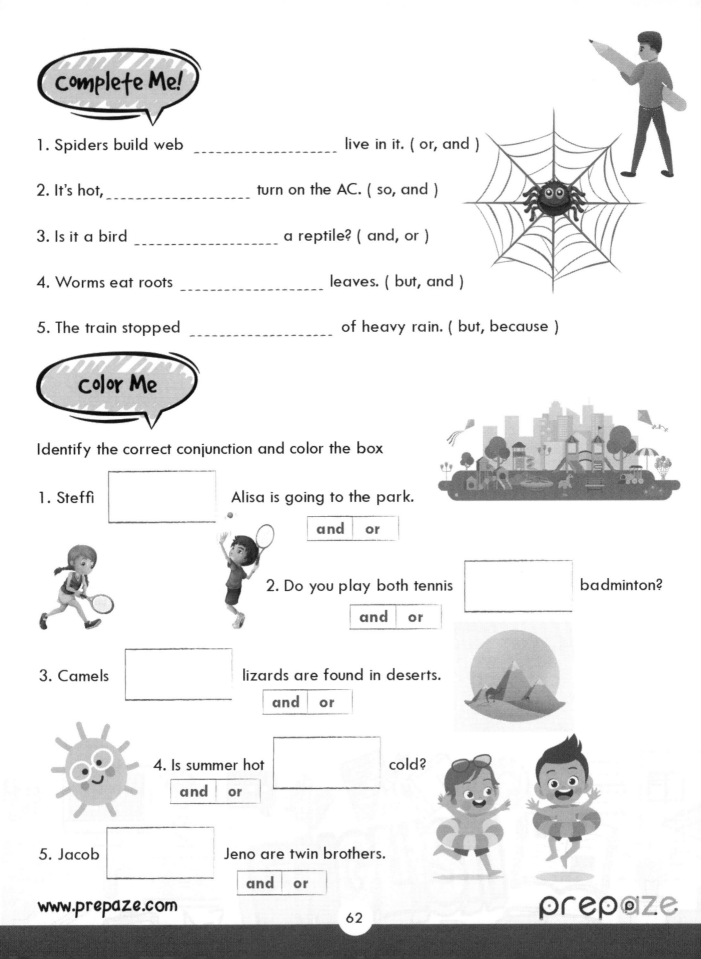

Complete Me!

1. Spiders build web _____ live in it. (or, and)

2. It's hot, _____ turn on the AC. (so, and)

3. Is it a bird _____ a reptile? (and, or)

4. Worms eat roots _____ leaves. (but, and)

5. The train stopped _____ of heavy rain. (but, because)

Color Me

Identify the correct conjunction and color the box

1. Steffi [ ] Alisa is going to the park.

   | and | or |

2. Do you play both tennis [ ] badminton?

   | and | or |

3. Camels [ ] lizards are found in deserts.

   | and | or |

4. Is summer hot [ ] cold?

   | and | or |

5. Jacob [ ] Jeno are twin brothers.

   | and | or |

Make Sentences

Write a sentence using the given conjunction.

and

so

but

or

Mark It with an X

Read the sentence. Mark the correct choice with an "X"

1. I like both English _____ math.

- (a) and
- (b) or
- (c) because
- (d) so
- (e) but

4. They bought both apples _____ oranges.

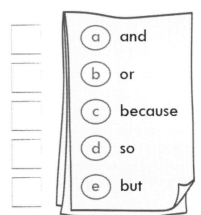

- (a) and
- (b) or
- (c) because
- (d) so
- (e) but

2. She has the flu, _____ she looks weak.

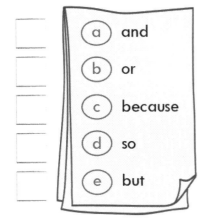

- (a) and
- (b) or
- (c) because
- (d) so
- (e) but

5. The house is new, _____ it leaks.

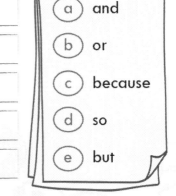

- (a) and
- (b) or
- (c) because
- (d) so
- (e) but

3. Is it _____ of the rain?

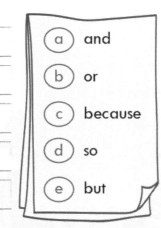

- (a) and
- (b) or
- (c) because
- (d) so
- (e) but

www.prepaze.com

64

prepaze

Determiners

These words are used before a noun
(name of a person, thing, or place).

Articles are: a, an, and the.

I have **a** cat.

This is **a** road.

I had **an** apple.

She is **an** expert.

The doctor is ready.

Please bring me **the** book.

Spot the Articles

Circle the articles in these sentences. One is done for you.

1. (The) ride is closed.

2. Are you a teacher?

3. She has an umbrella.

4. Martin travelled around the world.

5. Austin is a graduate.

6. He is in the ranch.

7. Shirley is a student.

8. The spider has eight legs.

9. Ralph is an honest man.

10. Frank needs a bike.

A or An?

Complete the sentences with articles "a" or "an."

1. _____ apple

2. _____ bird

3. _____ car

4. _____ bike

5. _____ umbrella

6. _____ banana

7. _____ orange

8. _____ student

9. _____ ink bottle

10. _____ doctor

Demonstrative Determiners

These words are used to point out a noun.

Examples: this, that, these, and those

This is an apple.

That is an apple.

These are apples.

Those are apples.

prepaze

Word Puzzle

Search the following determiners "an, the, this, that, these, and those."

c	x	p	i	h	n	o	t
k	s	r	e	h	t	n	i
w	a	n	j	m	h	y	b
t	r	l	c	x	i	d	l
h	n	t	h	e	s	e	j
o	v	h	y	q	b	r	z
s	e	c	o	k	c	v	d
e	t	e	s	t	h	a	t

This or That?

Choose the best answer

1. _____ is Julia. (These, This)

2. I know _____ boy. (those, that)

3. I bought _____ fruits for you. (these, that)

4. _____ apple was green. (That, These)

5. Place _____ chairs in line. (this, these)

6. She is good at _____ trick. (those, that)

7. _____ books are mine. (Those, That)

8. _____ is my pen. (This, Those)

9. _____ boys are from our baseball team. (These, That)

10. _____ girl goes to my school. (Those, That)

Look at the pictures and complete the puzzle accordingly.

Math

Use this book to enable your children to explore numbers by solving interesting puzzles and real-life problems. Engage your children with fun, colorful activities and let them fall in love with Math.

Putting Together

Addition

The process of combining one or more quantities is called addition.

Example

There are 3 balls in box 1 and 2 balls in box 2. On combining the balls in both boxes, we get 5 balls.

The process of combining one or more quantities is called addition.

We count forward to add the quantities.

We use the symbol '+' to represent addition.

Example, 3 balls + 2 balls = 5 balls

Addition is putting together.

1. Write a number sentence for each picture by counting the number of objects. The first one is done for you.

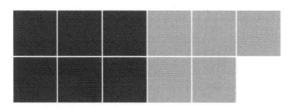

| 6 | + | 5 | = | 11 |

☐ + ☐ = ☐

☐ + ☐ = ☐

☐ + ☐ = ☐

How Many Items Does Angela Have?

2. Angela has the following items in her bag.

Pencil	4	
Crayons	10	
Books	3	

How many items does Angela have altogether?

3. Kevin has 2 avocado trees, 4 papaya trees, and 6 pear trees in his garden. How many trees does Kevin have in his garden?

Can You Make 10?

4. Say each number and color the number of boxes to match the number. How many more boxes would you need to color to make 10?

2									
5									
9									
6									
4									

5. Color the stars that make the number 5.

3+2   4+1   4+9

6. Solve the word problems.

a A duck has 2 legs. How many legs do 5 ducks have?

b There are 5 fingers in a hand. How many fingers are there in 2 hands?

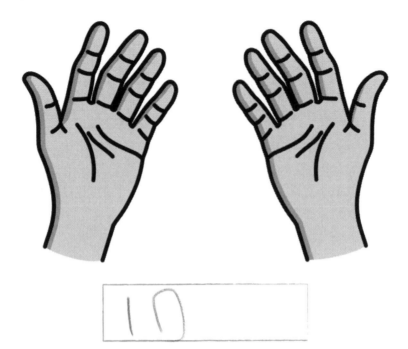

10

c There are 7 bees on a flower, 4 more join in. How many are there in all?

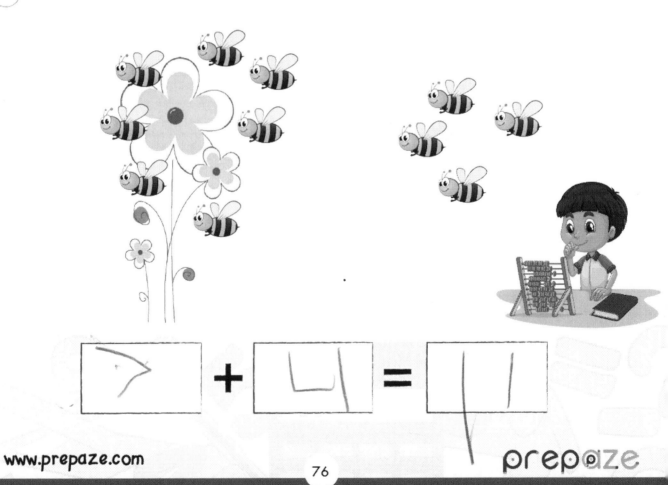

7 + 4 = 11

7. Mrs. Smith asked her 4 kids to bring some toys for the garage sale. The graph below shows the number of toys each kid brought.

■ No. of Toys

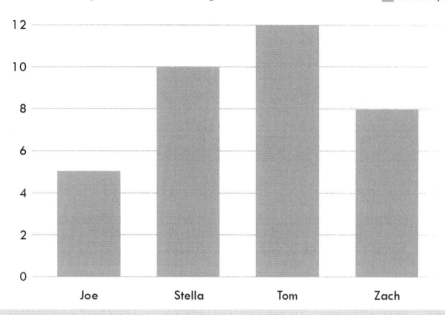

Write four different sentences to show how many toys were brought in all.

	+		+	
	+		=	

	+		+	
	+		=	

	+		+	
	+		=	

	+		+	
	+		=	

8. Draw the given number of balls and find their sum.

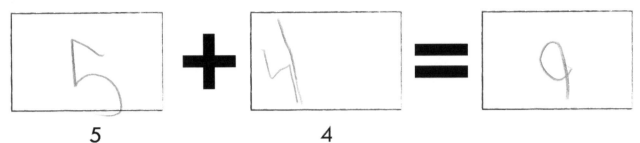

5   4

9. Use the numbers in the blanks and complete the number sentences.

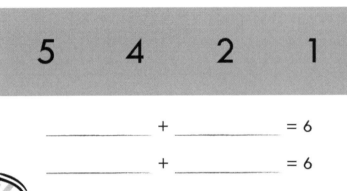

| 5 | 4 | 2 | 1 |

_____ + _____ = 6

_____ + _____ = 6

Joel's Marbles

10. Joel had 8 marbles and his friend Mario gave him 8 marbles. How many marbles does Joel have altogether?

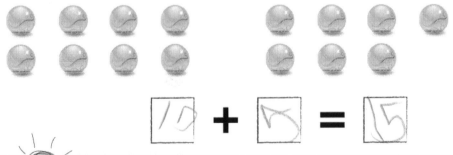

10 + 5 = 15

💡 **Do you know?**

Adding '0' to any number is the number itself?

Create 2 addition sentences with '0'

Taking Away

Subtraction

The process of taking away one quantity from another is called **subtraction**.

Example

There are 8 balls in a box. On taking away 5 balls from the box, we have 3 balls left.

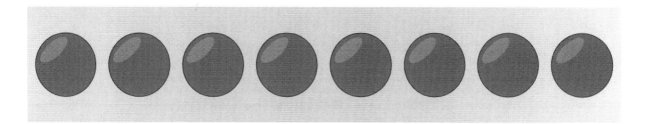

On taking away 5 balls from the box, we have 3 balls left.

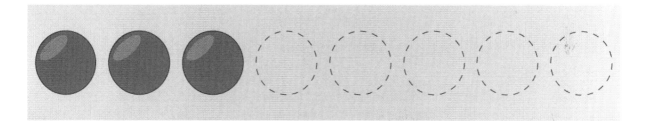

We count backward to subtract the quantities.

We use the symbol '−' to represent subtraction.

Example: 8 balls − 5 balls = 3 balls

1. Look at the picture and complete the story problem.

Farmer Joel harvested _____ carrots.

He gave away _____
carrots to his neighbors.

How many carrots does farmer Joel have now? _____

Puzzle Time

2. Complete the math puzzle by writing the numbers in sequence.

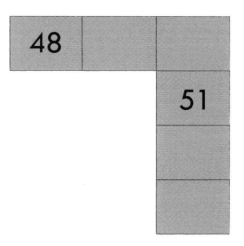

48		
		51

3. There are 20 sheep in a farm. The farmer sells 9 sheep. How many are there in the farm. Cross out the sheep to find the answer.

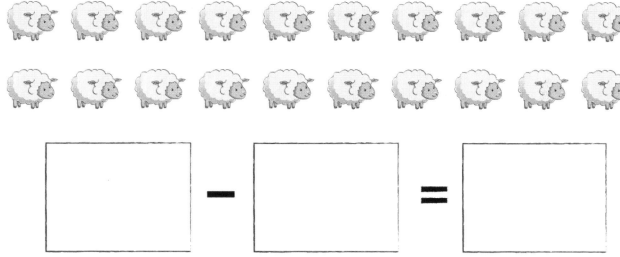

	−		=	

4. Write two subtraction sentences to arrive at the number 0.

a. _____ − _____ = 0

b. _____ − _____ = 0

prepaze

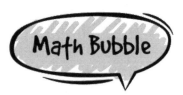

5. Subtract the numbers and write the answer in the bubble.

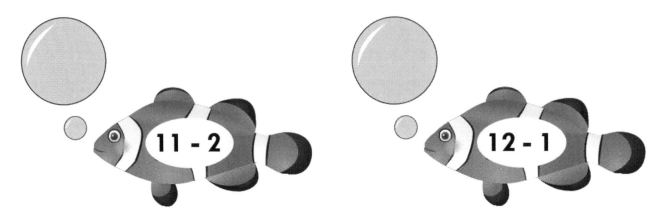

6. Use the number cards and make expressions that are equal to each other.

7	4	2	5

_____ − _____ = _____ − _____

7. Fill in the blanks.

a. 17 pens − 2 pens = _____ pens

b. 15 badges − 5 badges = _____ badges

c. 19 dolls − 4 dolls = _____ dolls

d. 16 fans − 3 fans = _____ fans

e. 18 boxes − 5 boxes = _____ boxes

8. Write the missing part.

Number Sense

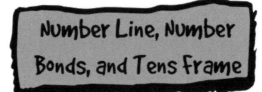

A **number line** helps to understand the relative position of a number and is a great tool for problem-solving. **Number bonds** help to split numbers and show how numbers can be joined together or how they can be broken down. **Ten-frames** are two rectangular frames split into ten parts in which objects like counters can be placed to understand the relationship between the numbers.

Let's Practice

1. Find the sum by coloring the tens frame.

10 + 4 = _____

10 + 9 = _____

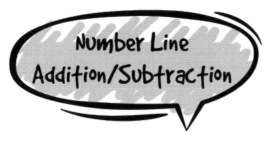

Number Line
Addition/Subtraction

2. Use the number line to add or subtract.

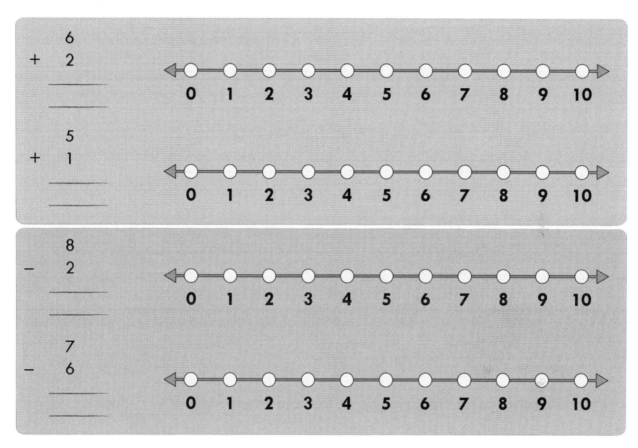

```
   6
+  2
_____
_____
```

```
   5
+  1
_____
_____
```

```
   8
-  2
_____
_____
```

```
   7
-  6
_____
_____
```

3. Work out the missing numbers in the rectangle by adding the numbers in the circles that join them.

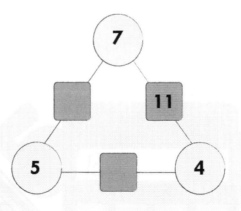

prepaze

4. 24 students are going to the farm. Then one more student decides to go. How many students will be at the farm? Use ten-frames to solve. Write and label your answer.

Match

5. Match the place value chart that shows the same number.

Tens	Ones
2	16

Tens	Ones
5	5

Tens	Ones
4	18

Tens	Ones
3	6

Tens	Ones
4	15

Tens	Ones
5	8

Let's Play a Math Game

Things you will need:

 Dice - 1

Counter / Lego blocks / or any small object in any two different colors - 1 each

Number line as shown.

0   1   2   3   4   5   6   7   8   9   10

How to play

1. Roll the dice.	
2. Place the object on the number line as the number on the dice.	0 1 2 3 4 5 6 7 8 9 10
3. Roll the dice again.	
4. Count forward by the number you just rolled and place the second object on the last count.	4 0 1 2 3 4 5 6 7 8 9 10
5. Write the addition statement.	3 + 4 = 7
Play the game as many times as you want.	

Understanding the relationship between numbers enables us to compare and order them.

Symbol	Comparative language
>	Greater than
<	Less than
=	Equal to

Let's Practice

1. Color the number in each set that is big.

10	9

8	6

7	1

4	5

0	2

3	10

2. Read the word problems and solve them.

a. Lydia and Susan both collected shells. Lydia collected 7 shells. Susan collected 4 shells. Who collected more shells?

Lydia   Susan

b. Stephanie read 10 pages on Monday and 6 pages on Tuesday. Which day did she read more pages?

Monday   Tuesday

3. Compare the number of objects in each box. Use symbols '>, <, ='
to explain your understanding.

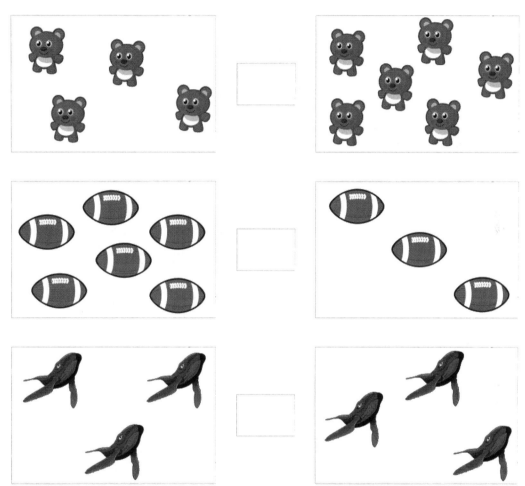

4. Write a number in each set that is smaller than the number given.

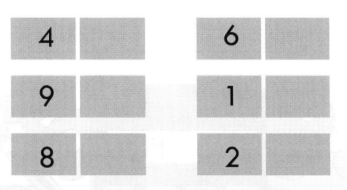

4		6	
9		1	
8		2	

Understanding Place Value

Every digit has a value based on its position in the number system and is defined as its **place value.** In the standard system, called **base ten,** each place has a value ten times to the value of the place to its right.

	1 block of **ones**		10 blocks of ones is 1 block of **tens**

Example

The number 26 can be represented in the place value system as 2 blocks of tens and 6 blocks of ones.

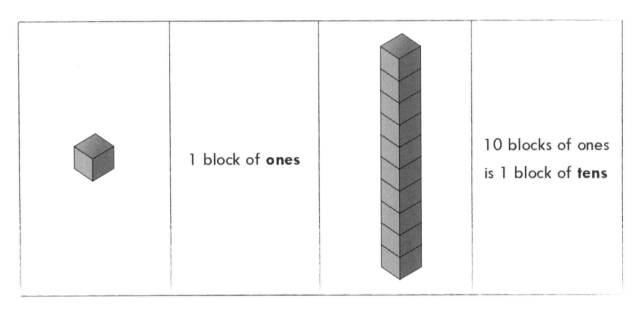

The place value system helps to understand the relationship between the place or position and the place value of the digits in a number.

prepaze

All About Cakes and Butterflies

1. Group the numbers as tens and ones. Fill in the place value table with the number of tens and ones.

a.

Tens	Ones

b.

Tens	Ones

2. Match the following bundles with the correct number.

2 tens   **4** ones

5 tens   **3** ones

1 tens   **3** ones

3. Match the following bundles with the correct number.

Numeral		Number Name
99		Nineteen
59		Fifty-nine
69		Eighty-nine
89		Ninety-nine
19		Sixty-nine

4. Make a number bond to show tens and ones

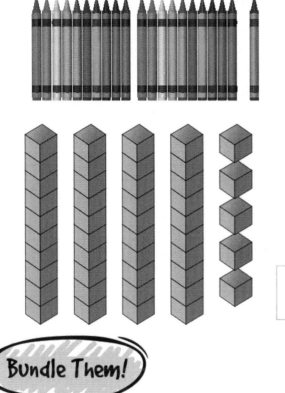

Bundle Them!

5. Draw bundles of tens and ones to represent the number.

a. 54

b. 31

c. 11

d. 39

6. Use the smileys below to answer the questions.

a. Color the first smiley yellow.

b. Color the eighth smiley red.

c. Color the fourth smiley green.

d. Color the fifth smiley pink.

e. If you color the last smiley, will it be the same as coloring the tenth smiley?

_____

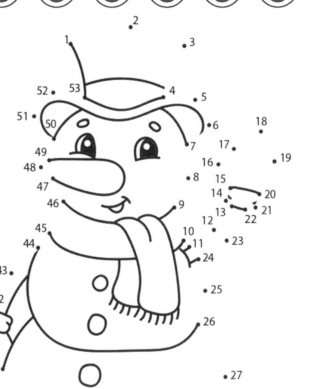

7. Connect the dots.

8. Color the correct number names for the given numeral.

a.	15	Fifty-one
		Fifteen
		One five
b.	88	Eighty-eight
		Eight eight
		Eight
c.	62	Twenty-six
		Six two
		Sixty-two

Comparison of Numbers

1. Write the number of objects in the blanks provided. Compare the two numbers and circle the greater number.

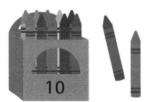   10      10

a. _____   _____

b. _____   _____

2. Write the number of objects in the blanks provided. Compare the two numbers and circle the smaller number.

a. _____   _____

b. _____   _____

3. Fill in the blanks with the correct number. Use the tens and ones to find the number.

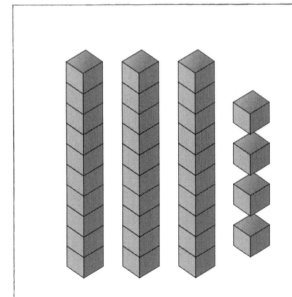 

10 more than 34 is _____   10 less than 46 is _____

Hundreds Chart

4. Use the hundreds chart to answer the questions.

a. What is 1 more than 89? _____

b. What is 1 less than 50? _____

c. What is 1 more than 20? _____

d. What is 1 more than 99? _____

e. What is 1 less than 9? _____

f. What is 10 more than 78? _____

g. What is 10 less than 55? _____

h. What is 3 less than 62? _____

i. What is 7 more than 43? _____

j. What is 10 less than 100? _____

1	2	3	4	5	6	7	8	9	10
11	12	13	14	15	16	17	18	19	20
21	22	23	24	25	26	27	28	29	30
31	32	33	34	35	36	37	38	39	40
41	42	43	44	45	46	47	48	49	50
51	52	53	54	55	56	57	58	59	60
61	62	63	64	65	66	67	68	69	70
71	72	73	74	75	76	77	78	79	80
81	82	83	84	85	86	87	88	89	90
91	92	93	94	95	96	97	98	99	100

Addition and Subtraction

Number Bonds

1. Complete the addition number bonds.

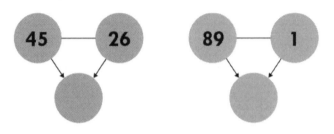

What Is Jack's favorite Game?

2. Solve the problems below. Use the alphabet code to answer the riddle.

What is Jack's favorite game?

43 + 10	99 + 1	60 – 50	0 + 10	15 + 15	28 + 11

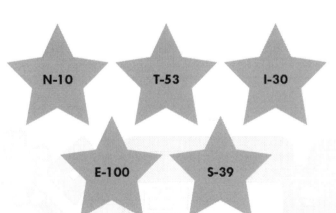

N-10   T-53   I-30

E-100   S-39

prepaze

3. Complete the subtraction number bonds.

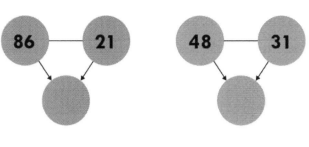

4. Use the RDW (Read, Draw, Write) process to solve the following problems.
Write the answer in the place value chart.

a. Emma is having a party for 24 of her friends. She already invited some friends.
She has 15 more invitations to send. How many friends has she already invited?

Tens	Ones

Emma already invited _____ friends.

b. Eva bought 9 red balls and 18 white balls. How many balls did she buy?

Tens	Ones

Eva bought _____ balls.

c. Olivia had 17 friends at her party. A few of them went outside to play on the trampoline. There were 4 friends remaining in the room. How many friends went outside?

Tens	Ones

_____ friends went outside.

d. On Monday, I bought 10 apples and on Tuesday I bought 15 apples. How many apples did I buy in all?

Tens	Ones

I bought _____ apples.

Number Equation

5. Write the number of balls in each box and complete the number equation using the correct symbols.

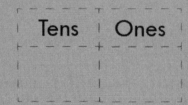

☐ _____ ☐ = ☐

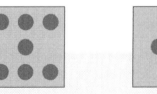

☐ _____ ☐ = ☐

6. Match the correct answer:

one more than	Number	fact
9	4	8 + 2
2	10	8 − 1
3	3	9 − 5
6	9	2 + 1
8	7	5 + 4

7. Color the pairs using different colors for each pair.

8 − 5	3 + 9
9 + 3	6 + 7
4 + 2 + 7	9 − 6
7 + 8	8 − 2
10 − 4	8 + 7

Measurement and Data

Measuring Length

Length is a measure of how long or short an object is. Length can be measured using non-standard units, such as, handspan, leg span, other smaller objects, etc., and standard tools, such as ruler, yardstick, measuring tape, etc.

Let's Practice

How Many Squares?

1. How many squares long is each object?

a. The pencil is _____ squares long.

b. The stick is _____ squares long.

2. Match the measuring tool that you would use to measure the following objects

Measuring Tool
Ruler
Measuring tape
Meter Stick

object
Your height
Pencil
Book

Arrange

3. Arrange the following from the tallest to the shortest.

a.

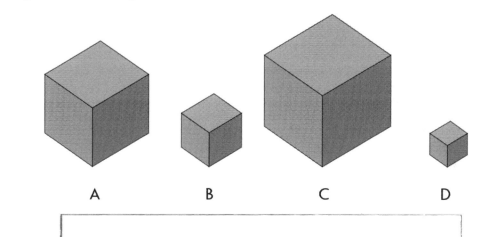

A   B   C   D

b.

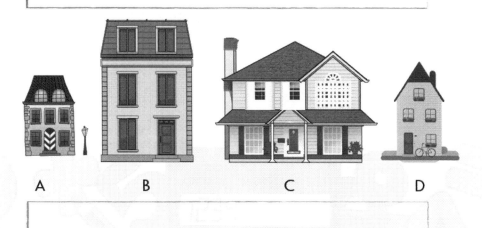

A   B   C   D

Help Zoe find
the Taller Tower

4. Help Zoe Find the Taller Tower.

Which tower is taller?

☐ Gray

☐ White

Tower _____ is taller than tower _____

by _____ blocks.

Which tower is taller?

☐ Gray

☐ White

Tower _____ is taller than tower _____

by _____ blocks.

5. There are 2 paths from Jack's house to reach the playground. Path A is shown in dotted lines and Path B in straight lines.

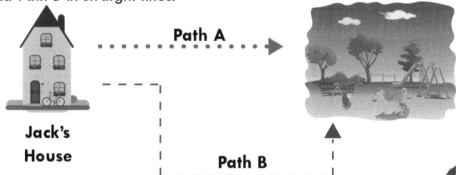

Path A is the _____ path and Path B is the _____ path.

Longer or Shorter?

6. Using a ruler, measure and write the length of each crayon and answer the questions.

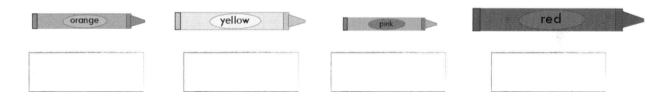

a. Which is the longest crayon? _____

b. Which is the shortest crayon? _____

c. Which crayon is longer than the pink crayon but shorter than the red crayon?

_____

d. Which crayons are shorter than the yellow crayon?

_____

7. Circle, color, or cross!

color the tallest	circle the shortest
circle the longest	cross the tallest

8. Measure the length of each of the common household items, using a paper clip. Then find the actual length using a ruler.

object	Length using paper clip	Length using ruler
Spoon		.
Table		
Pencil		

9. Which of the following will hold more water? Color it in blue.

Explain your answer _____

_____

10. Circle the object that is longest in each set.

11. Long or short?

a. Which is longer?

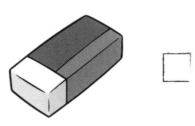   

b. Which is shorter?

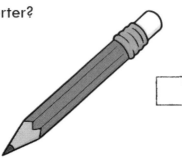   

Do you know the correct way to Measure?

12. Which picture shows the correct way to measure the triangle? And why?

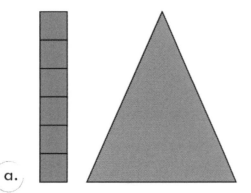   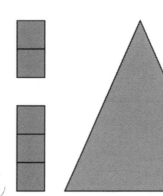   

a.   b.

The correct picture is _____

Why? _____

Help Steve and Rose

13. Solve the word problems.

a. Steve has a piece of cloth that is 5m long. Angela has a piece of cloth that is 10m long. Who has the shortest piece of cloth? By how much is it shorter than the other?

b. Rose places 7 pineapples one on top of the other. Lydia places 5 apples one on top of the other. Whose tower of fruits will be taller. Draw a picture to explain your answer.

14. Circle the biggest shape in each set below.

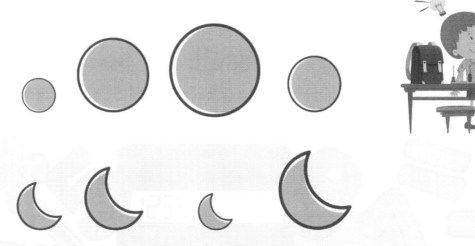

15. Circle the smallest shape in each set below.

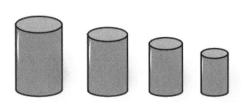

Let's Play a Math Game

1. Use a notebook to measure the height of different people at home.

a. I am _____ notebooks tall.

b. My mother/father is _____ notebooks tall.

c. My _____ is _____ notebooks tall.

d. I am _____ than my mother/father by _____ notebooks.

Can you measure with paperclips?

2. Use paperclips to measure the bars below. Fill in the blanks.

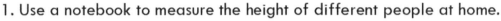

I used _____ paperclips to measure the purple bar.

I used _____ paperclips to measure the red bar.

I used _____ paperclips to measure the green bar.

I used _____ paperclips to measure the yellow bar.

Measuring Time

The day has different parts.

When the Sun appears to rise, it is called **morning.**

When the Sun is directly over our head, it is **noon.**

When the Sun appears to set, it is called **evening.**

When the Sun is not seen in the sky and is dark, it is **night.**

The position of the Sun helps to know the part of the day.

A clock is used to tell the accurate part of the day. A clock has 12 numbers and 2 hands. The longer hand is called the **minute hand,** and the smaller hand is called the **hour hand.**

Let's Practice

1. Connect each clock to its matching time.

   7: 00

          12: 00

          3: 00

   5: 00

2. Draw the hands on each clock to match the time written below.

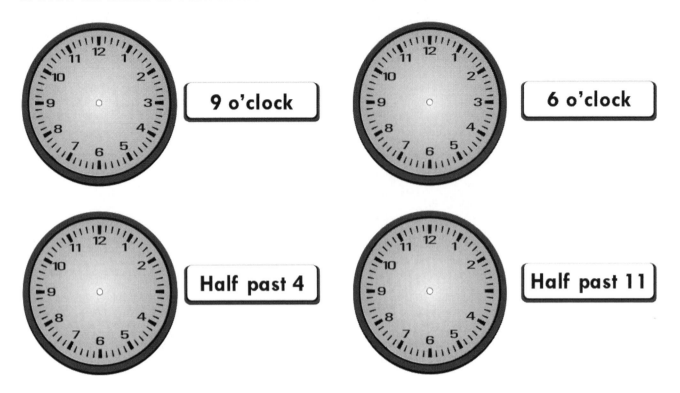

9 o'clock

6 o'clock

Half past 4

Half past 11

3. Solve the word problems.

a. Jennifer goes shopping at 10 o'clock. She comes back home exactly after an hour. How do the hands of the clock, one hour after 10 o'clock, look like? Circle the correct option.

b. Jimmy's school starts at 9:30. But he reaches school one hour before. How do the hands of the clock, one hour before 9:30, look like? Circle the correct option.

4. How long will each activity take? Circle the correct option.

Playing basketball with friends in the evening

About a minute   About an hour

Drawing and coloring a picture

About a minute   About an hour

Pouring water in a glass

About a minute   About an hour

Tying a shoelace

About a minute   About an hour

Calendar Problem

5. Use the calendar below to answer the following questions.

FEBRUARY

M	T	W	T	F	S	S
		1	2	3	4	5
6	7	8	9	10	11	12
13	14	15	16	17	18	19
20	21	22	23	24	25	26
27	28					

a. How many days are there in this month? _____

b. Jimmy's soccer match is on the 7th day of this month. What day of the week is it?

_____

c. Jaison's grandfather will be coming on the 4th Saturday of this month. Write the date.

_____

6. Read the word problems given below. Circle the correct time.

a) Everyday Rooney waits for his breakfast at this time.

b) Thomas gets ready for his school at this time.

c) Mike generally has his lunch at this time.

7. Read each clock and write the time. One is done for you.

	Hour hand is between **12** and **1** Minute hand is at **6** Time is **12:30**
	Hour hand is between _____ and _____ Minute hand is at _____ Time is _____
	Hour hand is between _____ and _____ Minute hand is at _____ Time is _____
	Hour hand is between _____ and _____ Minute hand is at _____ Time is _____
	Hour hand is between _____ and _____ Minute hand is at _____ Time is _____

prepaze

8. Draw a line to connect each digital clock to its matching time.

Half past 1

Half past 8

10 o'clock

Half past 6

Alarm Time!

9. Look at the time in each digital clock. Show the same time in the alarm clock by drawing the hour and minute hands.

Data can be collected, organized, and interpreted using various methods. A few methods are tables, tally marks, pictographs, and bar graphs.

Let's Practice

Which Is the favorite fruit of Ms.Rosy's class?

1. The students of Ms.Rosy's class had a vote for their favorite fruit. She made a picture graph with the results. Observe the graph and answer the questions.

Mangoes	🥭 🥭 🥭 🥭 🥭 🥭
Apples	🍎 🍎 🍎 🍎
Bananas	🍌 🍌 🍌 🍌 🍌
Cherries	🍒 🍒 🍒 🍒
Strawberries	🍓 🍓 🍓 🍓

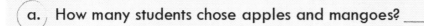

a. How many students chose apples and mangoes? _____

b. Which is the most popular fruit? _____

c. How many more classmates preferred bananas over cherries? _____

d. How many students are there in Ms.Rosy's class? _____

2. The teacher of Grade 1 took a vote on the student's favorite colors and she graphed the results. Use the bar graph to answer the questions.

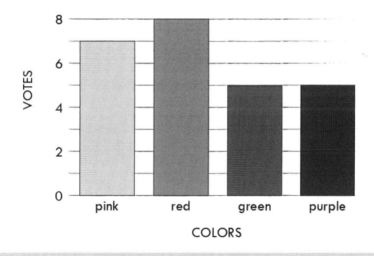

a. How many more students chose red than green? _____

b. How many more students voted for pink than purple? _____

c. Which two colors had the same number of votes? _____

d. List the colors in the order from the most number of votes to the least number of votes.

_____

World of Sea Animals

3. Color the graph according to the tally marks.

|||| || |||| ||||| |

8								
7								
6								
5								
4	▨							
3	▨							
2	▨							
1	▨							

4. Count the dots on the dominoes. Complete the table and then answer the following questions.

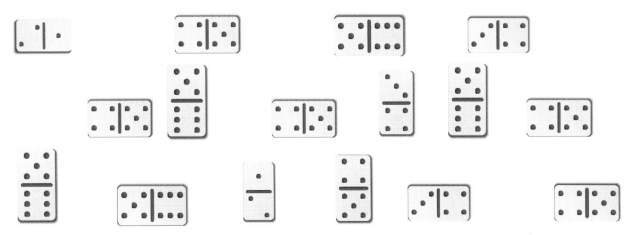

Table

3 Dots	**7 Dots**	**9 Dots**	**11 Dots**

a. Are there more dominoes with 9 or 11 dots? _____

b. How many dominoes with 7 dots are there? _____

c. How many more dominoes with 9 than 7 dots are there? _____

d. How many dominoes with 7 dots and 11 dots are there? _____

Which Movie to Watch?

5. The bar graph shows the preferred movies among the residents of Tenny City. Use the bar graph to answer the questions.

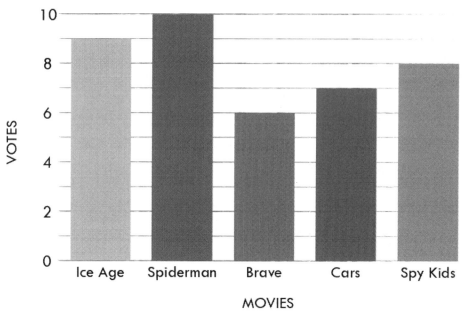

a. Which movie got more votes, Cars or The Ice Age? _____

b. Which is the most popular movie? _____

c. How many people voted for Spy Kids and Spiderman altogether? _____

d. What is the difference in the number of people who voted for Brave and the number of people who voted for Spy Kids?

_____

prepaze

6. James loves to grow vegetables in the garden. The picture graph shows the vegetables he harvested in his garden in a week. Use the information to answer the questions.

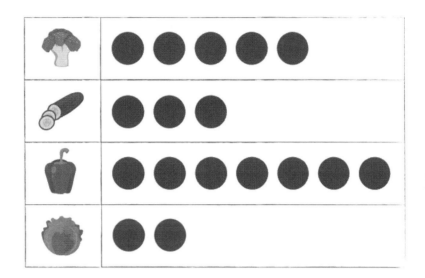

a. How many cucumbers did James harvest? _____

b. How many broccoli and lettuce did James harvest? _____

c. How many more bell peppers than cucumber did James harvest? _____

d. How many vegetables did James harvest altogether? _____

7. Ms.Molly made a bar graph on favorite pets of her class students. Use the bar graph to answer the questions.

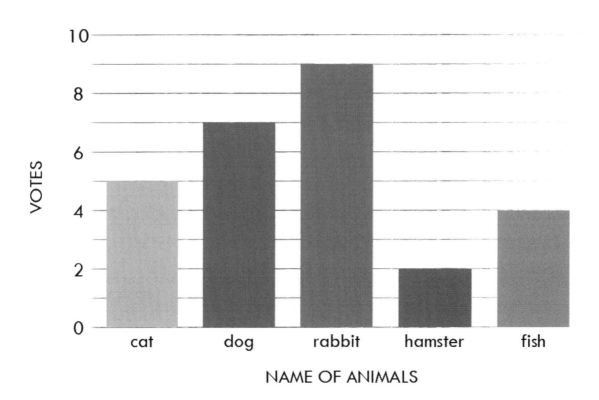

NAME OF ANIMALS

a. Which pet got the least votes?_____

b. Which pet got the most votes?_____

c. How many votes did the rabbit get?_____

d. How many more votes did the dog get over cat?_____

8. The picture graph shows the sport preference of Grade 1 students at Valley School. Use the graph to answer the questions.

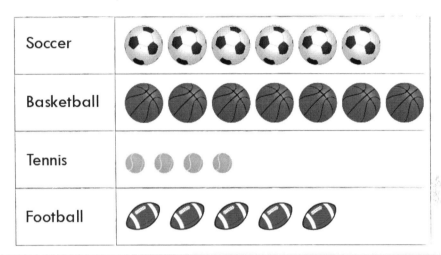

a. How many students like basketball the most? _____

b. Which is the most popular sport? _____

c. How many students do not like tennis the most? _____

d. How many students prefer football over tennis? _____

e. Is the number of students who like soccer the same as the number of students who like football?

_____

9. Jaison and his friends made a graph based on the weather forecast of a particular week. Use the bar graph to answer the questions.

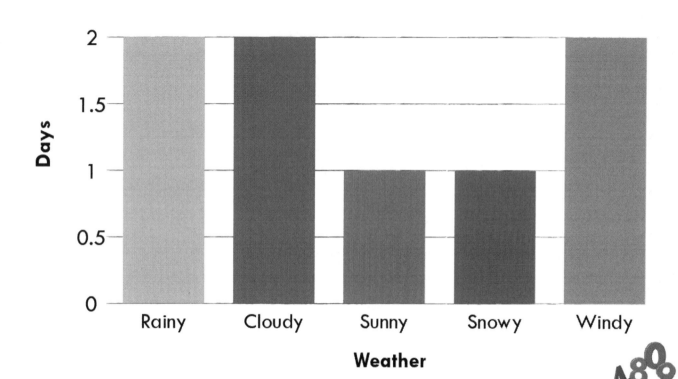

a. How many days were cloudy?_____

b. How many days were windy?_____

c. How many days were sunny? _____

d. Were there more rainy days or more snowy days? _____

A Cakelicious Problem!

10. The following pictograph shows the number of cake pieces John, Eva, Olivia, and Richard ate on Christmas. Use the graph to answer the questions.

John	🍰🍰🍰🍰
Eva	🍰🍰🍰🍰🍰
Olivia	🍰🍰🍰🍰
Richard	🍰🍰🍰🍰🍰🍰

a. Who ate only three cake pieces? _____

b. Two of them ate the same number of cake pieces. Who are they? _____

_____

c. How many cake pieces did John and Eva eat altogether? _____

d. Who ate one cake piece less than Richard? _____

11. The pictograph shows the number of toys sold on a sale day. Use the information to answer the questions.

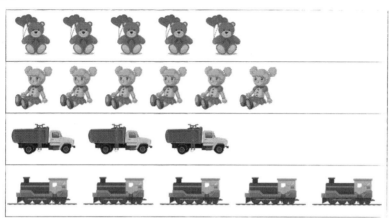

a. Which toy was sold the least? _____

b. How many dolls were sold? _____

c. How many more teddy bears were sold than the toy trucks? _____

d. How many toy trains and toy trucks were sold altogether? _____

12. Count the objects, write the tally marks in the space provided.

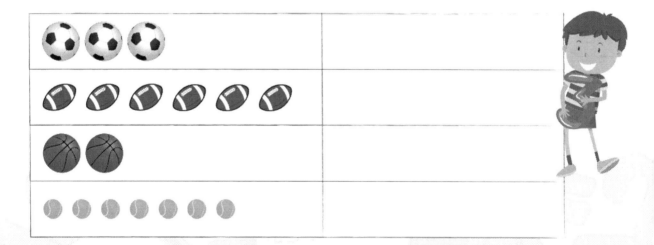

13. Count the vegetables and represent the count on the bar graph.

 1 Tomato    6 Fresh Beans   3 Mushrooms

 2 Carrots   3 Bell Peppers   7 Asparagus

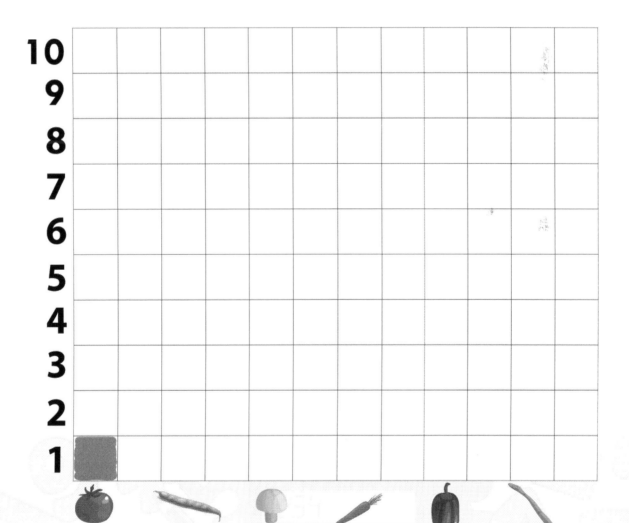

Geometry

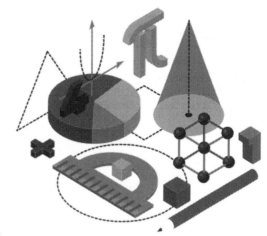

Geometry is about shapes and their attributes. Every shape has different attributes.

Triangle, square, rectangle, and pentagon are called regular polygons. They have corners and sides. Circle is a curved shape, it does not have any corner and has one side. Polygons and circles are also called as 2 D shapes.

Let's Practice

Corners and Sides

1. Write the number of corners and straight sides that each shape has.

_____ corners   _____ sides

_____ corners   _____ sides

_____ corners   _____ sides

_____ corners   _____ sides

Circle Them Up!

2. a. Circle one-third of the apples.

b. Circle one-fourth of the candies.

c. Circle one-half of the stars.

3. A square has 4 corners and 4 straight sides. Cross off the one that is not a square.

Explain your thinking

_____

_____

4. Look at the shapes below. Do they have equal parts? Circle 'Equal' if they have equal parts. Circle 'Unequal' if they have unequal parts.

Equal

Unequal

Equal

Unequal

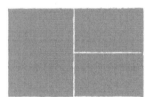

Equal

Unequal

Equal

Unequal

Equal

Unequal

Equal

Unequal

Equal

Unequal

Equal

Unequal

5. Which shape would we get if we join two squares? Draw and label the shape.

6. Divide the objects into two equal parts. Color half of each group. One is done for you.

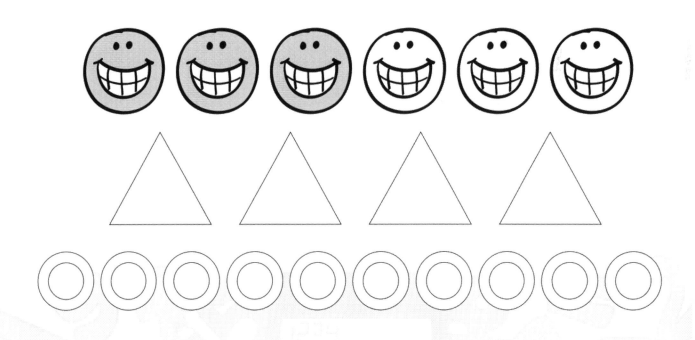

Share the oranges!

7. Alison, Eva, and Sasha all like oranges. Share the oranges equally among them.

Alison	Eva	Sasha

Bake a Pizza

8. Mark is making a pizza for his family. Follow the directions to help Mark make his pizza.

a. Divide the pizza into 4 equal parts.

b. Add sauce to the whole pizza.

c. Add cheese to half of the pizza.

d. Add onions to the other half of the pizza.

e. Add pepperoni to one-third of the pizza.

f. Add corn to one-fourth of the pizza.

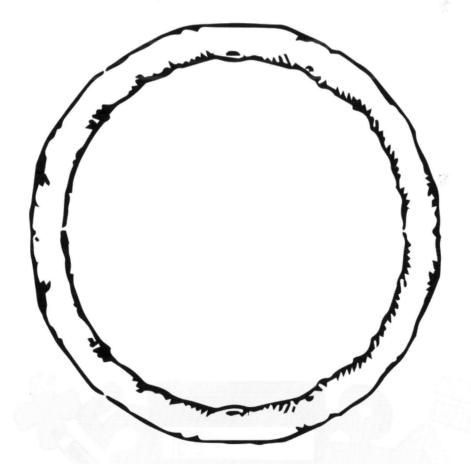

9. Circle the polygons in the given set of shapes.

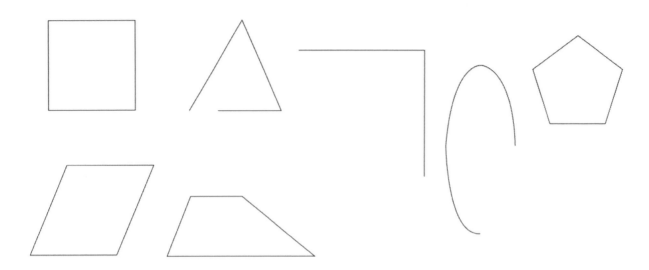

Tangram Boat

10. Identify the shapes in a tangram, then fill the boat with those shapes.

Sample tangram.

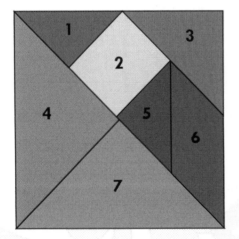

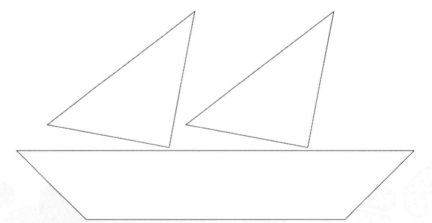

11. Match the shapes with the corresponding objects.

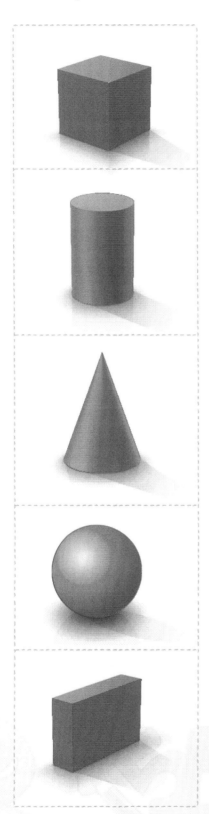
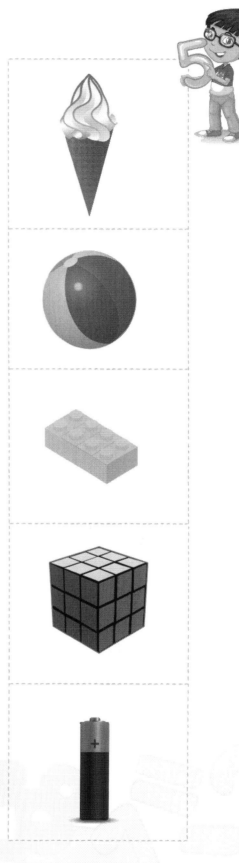

prepaze

12. Color the 3D shapes that make the shape given

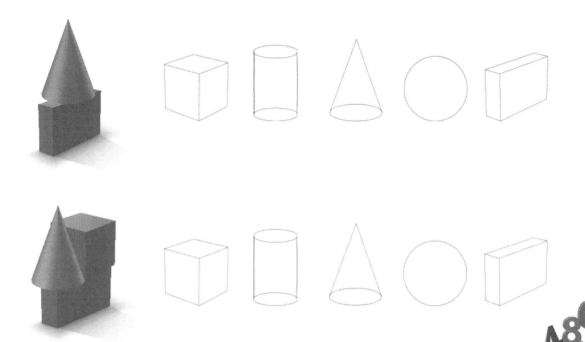

13. How can you divide the pizza into 4 equal parts?

prepaze

14. Circle the non polygons in the given set of shapes.

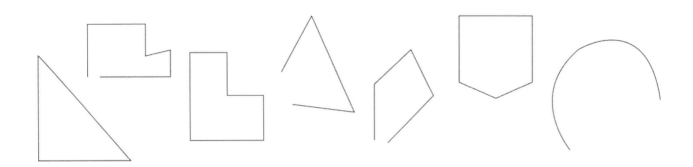

15. This bird is made of two shapes. Count each shape and write it in the space provided.

16. Draw a line to divide each figure into two equal halves.

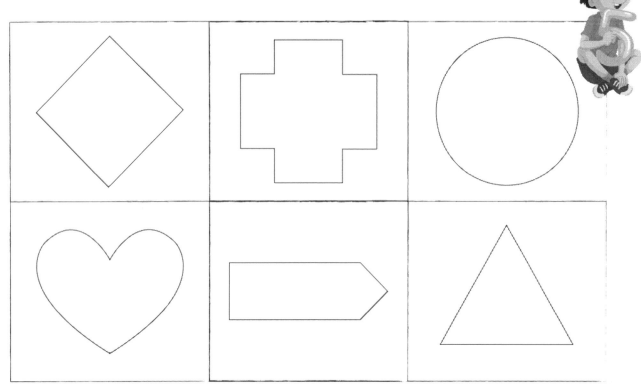

Pattern

17. Continue the pattern given using the shapes

18. Can we place a cube on the tip of a cone? Choose the correct answer.

YES   NO

Explain your thinking

_____

_____

_____

_____

19. Draw lines to make 6 equal parts. What smaller shapes did you make?

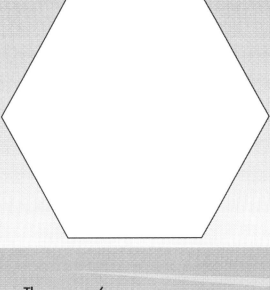

There are 6 _____ shapes.

20. Divide the following figures into two equal parts.

Share and Care!

21. Follow the instruction to answer the questions below.

a. Share 8 carrots between 2 rabbits equally.

b. Share 9 candies among 3 friends equally

Steve	Marcus	Joe

22. Circle the shapes that have 4 straight sides.

Riddle Time!

23. Follow the instruction to answer the questions below.

a. I am a closed shape with no corners and no straight sides. Who am I? Draw the shape in the box.

b. I am a closed shape with 3 corners and 3 straight sides. Who am I? Draw the shape in the box.

c. I am a closed shape with 5 corners and 5 straight sides. Who am I? Draw the shape in the box.

d. I am a closed shape with 4 corners and 4 sides with only two sides of the same length. Who am I? Draw the shape in the box.

24. Color all the shapes with only curved sides.

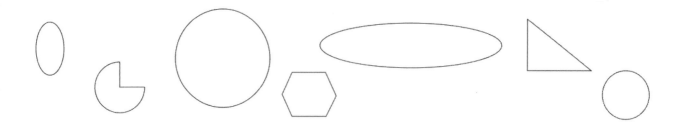

25. Circle the words that are the defining attribute of a pentagon.

It has 5 sides   It is big

It is a closed shape

It is red in color   It has 5 corners

26. a. What attributes are the same for all the shapes in Group A.

"Group A"

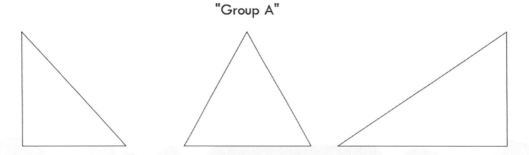

The shapes have _____ sides

The shapes have _____ corners

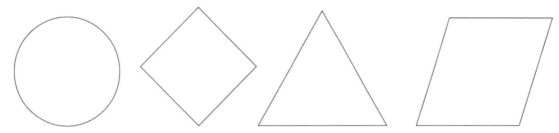

c. Draw two more shapes that would fit in Group A.

d. Draw one shape that would not fit in Group A.

27. Match the shape with their names.

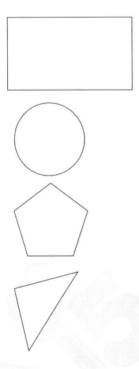

circle

Pentagon

Triangle

Rectangle

prepaze

28. Look at the square, it is filled by a shape. Circle that shape in the box.

29. Look at the following shapes. Choose the pair that is made up of the same shapes.

30. There are two triangles given. Fill each triangle using different shapes.

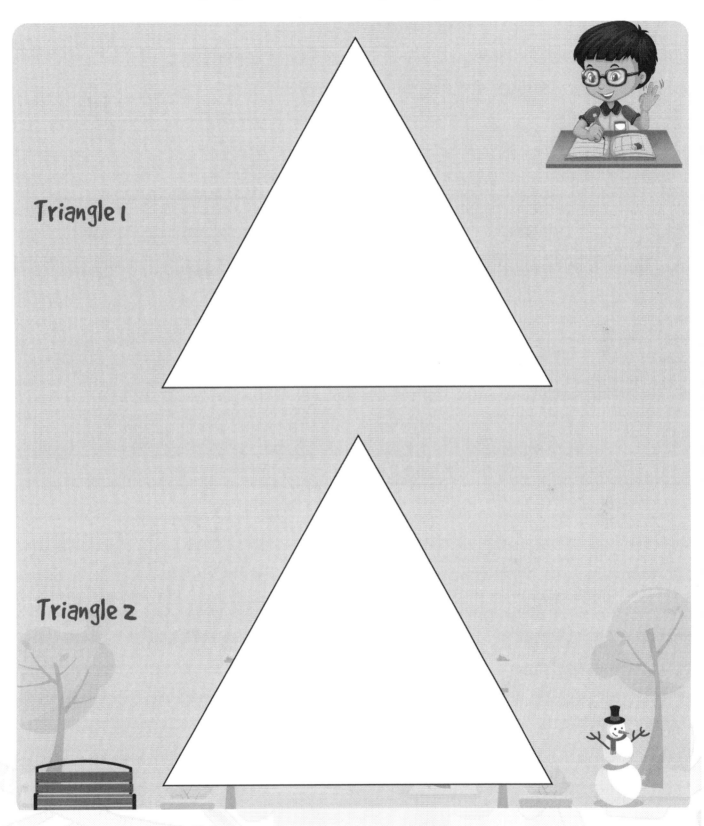

Triangle 1

Triangle 2

Let's play a Math Game

There are many shapes that we see around us. Draw one object each for each of these given shapes and write the name of the object.

Square	
	_____
Circle	
	_____
Rectangle	
	_____

Magic Square Puzzle is a puzzle which involves placing digits in the correct places so that each row, column and diagonal adds up to the same number.

1. Write the numbers 1, 1, 2, 2, 3, 3 correctly so that each line adds up to 6.

2. Write the numbers 3, 3, 4, 4, 5, 5 correctly so that each line adds up to 12.

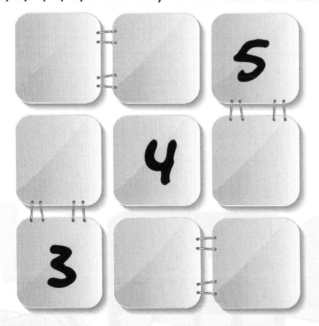

Science

Help your children learn and enjoy a wide range of information and fun facts that will surprise and amaze them. Find numerous Science experiments, cool facts, activities, and quizzes for the children to enjoy learning.

Physical Sciences

States of Matter

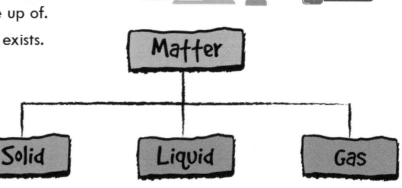

Matter is what all things are made up of. There are 3 forms in which matter exists.

Solids, liquids, and gases have different properties. These properties can change when the substances are mixed, cooled, or heated.

```
            Matter
    ┌──────────┼──────────┐
  Solid      Liquid       Gas
```

Solid	matter that has a definite shape
Liquid	matter that takes up the shape of the container it is in
Gas	matter that spreads out to fill the container it is in

Solid, Liquid, or Gas

Identify the form of each object as solid, liquid, or gas.

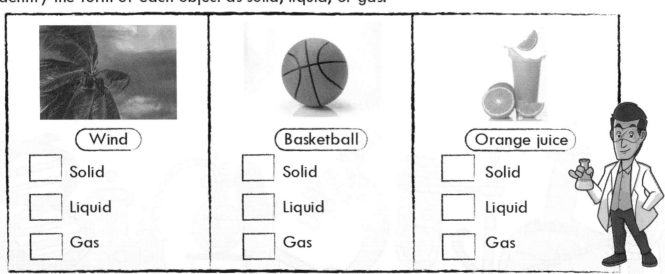

Wind
- ☐ Solid
- ☐ Liquid
- ☐ Gas

Basketball
- ☐ Solid
- ☐ Liquid
- ☐ Gas

Orange juice
- ☐ Solid
- ☐ Liquid
- ☐ Gas

Milk
- [ ] Solid
- [ ] Liquid
- [ ] Gas

Chocolate
- [ ] Solid
- [ ] Liquid
- [ ] Gas

Fume
- [ ] Solid
- [ ] Liquid
- [ ] Gas

Forms of Matter

Categorize the given objects based on their forms of matter.

exhaust	juice	orange	steam
soda	milk	brick	oxygen
pencil	smoke	table	wood
rain	snow	smoke	ketchup

Solids

Liquids

Gases

 **States of Matter**

Draw two objects for each of the forms and write their names.

Solids

Liquids

Gases

Properties of Matter

 Step 1 Identify one of each solid, liquid, and gas in your house.

Solid: _____

Liquid: _____

Gas: _____

Step 2 Draw the identified objects in the table given below.

Step 3 Complete the table by placing a ✔ mark for the properties that are applicable to each object and a ✗ mark for those that are not applicable.

Name of the property	Solid	Liquid	Gas
Example			
Is rigid	☐	☐	☐
Has shape	☐	☐	☐
Can flow	☐	☐	☐
Spreads out evenly	☐	☐	☐
Is visible	☐	☐	☐
Can be felt	☐	☐	☐
Can be squished	☐	☐	☐
How many check marks?			

The placement of **particles** in an object decides its form. If the particles are tightly packed, the object is a **solid**. If the particles are loosely packed, the object is a **liquid**. In a **gas**, the particles are freely dispersed.

Most materials can change from one form to another when they are heated, cooled, or mixed.

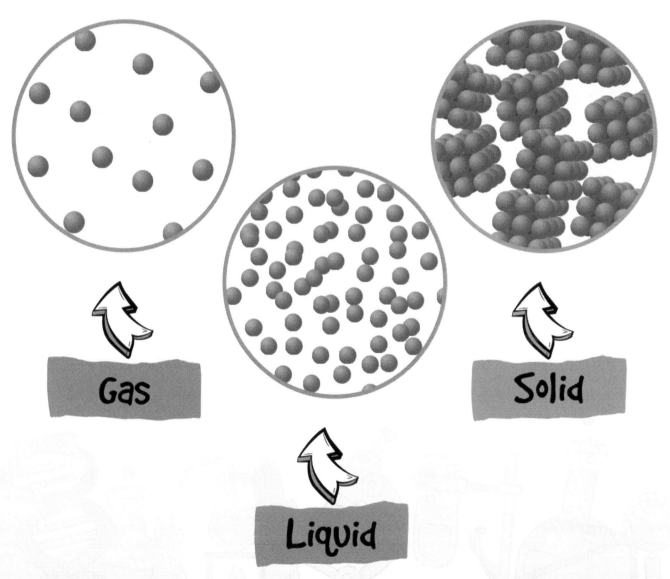

Gas

Liquid

Solid

Scavenger Hunt

Time for a scavenger hunt! Walk around your house, and categorize the different things you find based on their state of matter.

Solid	Liquid	Gas

Answer the following questions.

1. Which state of matter did you find the most? _____

2. Which state of matter did you find the least? _____

prepaze

True or False

State whether the following statements are true or false.

1. Only non-living things are called matter.

2. Water can be a solid, a liquid, and a gas.

3. Solids can change shape based on the container they are in.

4. Most gases cannot be seen.

5. Liquids expand to fill the container they are in.

6. Gases cannot flow.

7. All matter has mass.

8. There are 2 states of matter.

9. Solid occupies a definite space and feels hard when touched.

10. Liquids do not have a definite shape.

Changes in the States of Matter

Matter can change from one state to another when heated, cooled, or mixed. When matter changes from one state to another, its property also changes accordingly.

The various processes involved in change in states of matter are shown below.

ice (solid)

steam (gas)

water (liquid)

Effects of Heat on Matter

Match the following images to show what happens **when** they are heated.

Process of change in States

Answer the following questions by choosing the correct answer.

1. How do you make pancakes using batter?

☐   Heating

☐   Cooling

☐   Mixing

2. How do you make ice cubes using water?

☐   Heating

☐   Cooling

☐   Mixing

3. How do you bake a cake using batter?

☐   Heating

☐   Cooling

☐   Mixing

prepaze

4. How do you make a smoothie using fruits?

☐ Heating

☐ Cooling

☐ Mixing

5. How do you make popsicles using fruit extract?

☐ Heating

☐ Cooling

☐ Mixing

Word Grid

Spot the answers in the grid for the given clues.

1. To change from a solid to liquid.

2. To heat a liquid until it begins to change to gas.

3. To change from liquid to solid.

4. To remove heat away.

5. To change from liquid to gas.

F	A	H	M	T	G	P	U	J
R	J	V	S	C	U	D	K	M
E	V	A	P	O	R	A	T	E
E	G	N	V	O	P	M	B	L
Z	B	O	I	L	A	S	I	T
E	I	W	A	N	G	C	A	D

Chef of the Day

Put on your chef hat!

Find out the recipe for one of your favorite dishes and write it down here. Draw an image of the final dish.

Also mention the techniques you are using - heating, cooling, or mixing.

Be aware! Certain recipes may involve a combination of these techniques too!

Good luck!

Water and Heat

Complete the table.

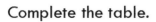	+	=	Name of the change: _____
	−	=	Name of the change: _____
	+	=	Name of the change: _____

Water cycle

Observe the diagram of the water cycle. Identify the changes in the states of matter and complete the table.

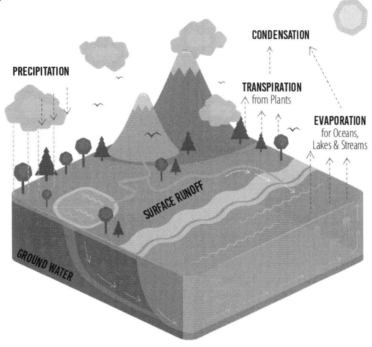

No	Previous Form	Current Form	Name of the Process
	Water from water bodies		
		Tiny droplets of water in clouds	
			Precipitation
			Transpiration

prepaze

Life Sciences

Parts of a Plant

Mark the parts of the plant and match with their uses.
Color the plant.

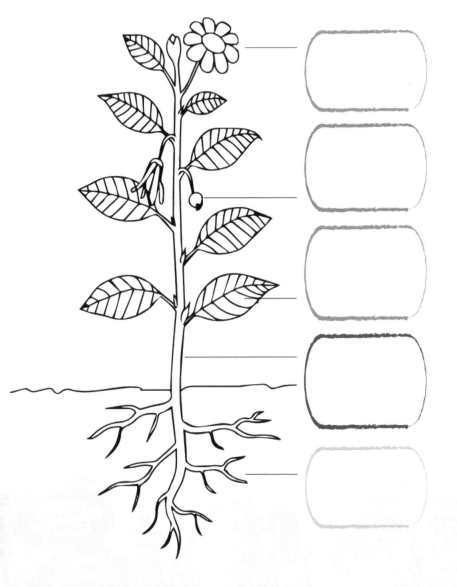

Holds the plant upright

Usually green and prepares the food for the plant

Absorbs water and nutrients from the soil

Helps the plants to produce seeds that grow into new plants

Many are good to eat and they protect the seeds

Alien Plants

Imagine a plant comes to Earth from space.

1. What do you think this alien plant will look like?

2. What super powers will you want the alien plant to have? Write any 2 here.

_____

_____

_____

Unity in Diversity of Animals

Circle the odd one out and write the criteria you used to choose the answer.

1. Criteria: _____

2. Criteria: _____

3. Criteria: _____

prepaze

4. Criteria: _____

5. Criteria: _____

6. Criteria: _____

Eating Habits of Animals

1. Categorize the animals given in the grid based on their eating habits.

cat	tiger	dog	cow	sheep
lion	panda	crow	bear	ant
bee	elephant	human	giraffe	wolf

Eats Plants	Eats Animals	Eats both Plants and Animals

2. Fill in the empty spaces with other animals you know of with a similar eating habit.

prepaze

Did You Know?

All living things can be classified as **plants** and **animals**.

That means, every organism is either a plant or an animal. For instance, while we know that a palm tree is a plant, parrot is an animal.

What do you think humans are classified as? Choose the correct answer.

☐ Plants

☐ Animals

Why do you think so?

Types of Animals

Mammals	animals with fur or hair on their body and give birth to young ones
Birds	animals that have feathers on their body
Insects	animals whose body has 3 segments with 6 legs
Reptiles	animals that have scales on their body and live on land
Fishes	animals that have scales on their body and live in water

If Animals Had an ID Card...

Complete the ID cards of the given animals.

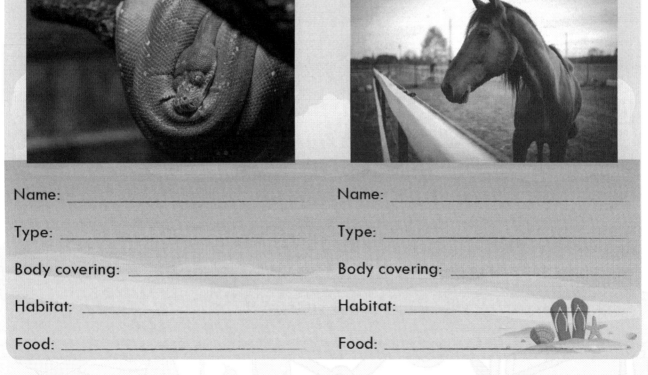

Name: _____   Name: _____

Type: _____   Type: _____

Body covering: _____   Body covering: _____

Habitat: _____   Habitat: _____

Food: _____   Food: _____

Name: _____

Type: _____

Body covering: _____

Habitat: _____

Food: _____

Name: _____

Type: _____

Body covering: _____

Habitat: _____

Food: _____

Name: _____

Type: _____

Body covering: _____

Habitat: _____

Food: _____

Name: _____

Type: _____

Body covering: _____

Habitat: _____

Food: _____

prepaze

Can Plants Live Without Light?

Let's do a simple experiment to check if plants need sunlight.

What you need:

 2 small potted plants

 1 carton box - big enough to cover a plant

How to do:

 **Step 1** Keep one potted plant in a well ventilated area like near a window.

 **Step 2** Take the other potted plant, keep it away from the window, and cover it with the carton.

 **Step 3** Water the plants regularly for a week.

 **Step 4** On the eighth day, uncover the carton and observe the condition of both the plants.

What do you infer:

1. Did you water both the plants?

☐   Yes

☐   No

2. Did both the plants get sunlight?

☐   Yes

☐   No

3. On the eighth day did both the plants appear to be healthy?

☐   Yes

☐   No

4. Why do you think the plant that was left covered did not look healthy?

_____

_____

_____

5. Which of these do you think is important for plants to grow?

☐   Sunlight

☐   Water

☐   Both

prepaze

How did the plants look before and after the activity? Illustrate.

Before:

After:

Conclusion

Hence, it is clear that plants need _____ to grow.

The Teeth Study

Identify the food of these animals by observing the structure of their teeth.

food chain

Number the organisms from 1 to 4 in the correct order to form a food chain.

1.

2.

3.

4. Write or draw your own food chain in the space provided.

1	2	3	4

characteristics of organisms

Complete the steps given below.

 **Step 1** Identify a plant and an animal.

Plant: _____

Animal: _____

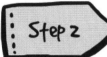 **Step 2** Draw the identified organisms in the table given below.

Step 3 Complete the table by placing a ✓ mark for the characteristics that are applicable to each organism and a ✗ mark for those that are not applicable.

	Plants	Animals
Example		
Movement The organism can move by themselves.	☐	☐
Respiration The organism breathes in oxygen and breathes out carbon dioxide.	☐	☐

	Plants	Animals
Sensitivity The organism can feel changes in their surroundings like heat and cold.	☐	☐
Growth The organism grows in size.	☐	☐
Reproduce The organism can produce young ones of its own kind.	☐	☐
Excrete The organism sends out the unwanted waste materials from the body.	☐	☐
Nutrition The organism eats and gets nutrients from other plants and animals.	☐	☐

 Did You Know?

No matter how many check marks and crosses you have placed, **all** living organisms, both plants and animals, exhibit each of the characteristics mentioned in the activity.

These 7 characteristics are common to all the organisms and are called **life processes.**

One quick way to remember these 7 processes is using the acronym - **MRS. GREN.**

Each of the characters represent one life process, in the same order as mentioned in the activity.

prepaze

Earth Sciences

Trace the names of the seasons and decorate the tree appropriately for each season.

summer

spring

winter

fall

1. Identify the different weather and write in the blank.

2. What does it look like outside? Circle today's weather in the above pictures.

Identify the Instruments

Identify the following instruments and explain their use.

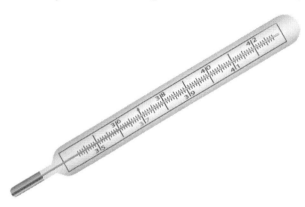

What is this instrument?

_____

What is it used for?

_____

_____

What is this instrument?

_____

What is it used for?

_____

_____

What is this instrument?

_____

What is it used for?

_____

_____

prepaze

DIY Wind Vane

Let's make a wind vane!

What you need:

- 1 paper plate
- A pair of scissors
- A poster board or chart paper
- A plastic straw
- A board pin
- A new pencil with eraser

- Modeling clay
- Glue
- A compass
- A styrofoam plate (optional)
- Some crayons (optional)

How to do:

Step 1 Write the names of the four directions on an inverted paper plate as shown here.

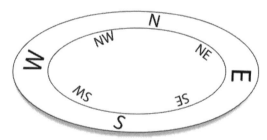

Step 2 You can personalise your wind vane by decorating this plate of your choice using crayons.

Step 3 Draw an arrow head and an arrow tail on the poster board about 2 inches in length. You can also trace the images given here. You could use the styrofoam plate to cut out these shapes.

Step 4

Make small slits at each end of the straw using the scissors for about quarter an inch. Insert the arrow head and the arrow tail in each of the slits and stick them using the glue. Once you are done, the straw will look like an arrow.

Step 5

Insert a pin through the center of the straw and into the eraser behind the pencil. Seek the help of an adult for this step, if necessary. Ensure the pin is not too tight on the straw and allows it to rotate freely. Note: If the straw arrow looks unbalanced, adjust the sizes of the arrowhead and arrow tail to balance it.

Step 6

Make a palm-size ball of the polymer clay. Insert the pencil-arrow setup into it. The ball of clay will act as a stand for the pencil and arrow and help it stay upright.

Step 7

Press the ball of clay along with the arrow setup on the paper plate that has directions written on it.

Step 8

Your wind vane is now ready. Identify the North using the compass, and adjust the north on the windvane to point in the correct direction. Once the wind blows, see the wind vane spin and align itself to the direction of the wind.

Step 9

Identify the direction of wind at different times during the day.

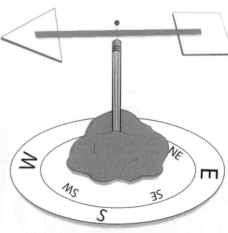

prepaze

Reading Thermometers

1. Write down the readings from the thermometers. One is done for you.

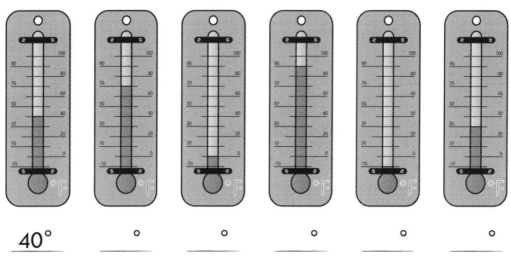

40°   °   °   °   °   °

2. Color the thermometers to show the correct readings.

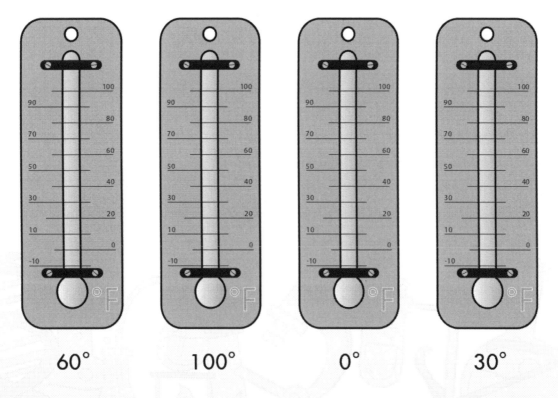

60°   100°   0°   30°

Weather Report

1. Refer your local newspaper or use the internet to find out the maximum and minimum temperatures for the last 10 days. Complete the table.

No.	Date	Day	Maximum Temperature	Minimum Temperature

Answer the following questions.

A. Is maximum temperature the same for all the days?

☐ Yes

☐ No

B. Is minimum temperature the same for all the days?

☐ Yes

☐ No

C. What is the weather like today? _____

D. What is the current season in your locality? _____

E. Do you think the temperature will be the same during a different season?

☐ Yes

☐ No

F. Give reasons for your answer in E:

_____

_____

_____

prepaze

Seasons and Weather

1. Draw lines to match the weather with the seasons.

SUMMER

WINTER

SPRING

FALL

Note: Every season may have one or more weather mapped to it.

Seasons and Apparels

Categorize the apparels according to the seasons.

Summer	Spring	Fall	Winter

boots	trousers	scarf	cardigan	flip flops	cap
vest	coat	jeans	shirt	sandals	jumper
tights	shorts	socks	skirt	bikini	woolly hat
dress	sun glasses	t-shirt	shoes	tracksuit	jacket

Favorite Season

1. Which is your favorite season? _____

2. Color the scenery in line with your answer.

Weather in your Locality

Refer to minimum and maximum temperature reading and identify the weather for the last 10 days from page 186. Draw the corresponding logo for each weather.

Sunny

Cloudy

Rainy

Windy

Snowy

Stormy

No	Date	Day	What's the weather?

prepaze

Investigation and Experimentation

Observe the bar graph given and answer the following questions.

The students of grade 1 vote for their favorite fruit. Here are the results.

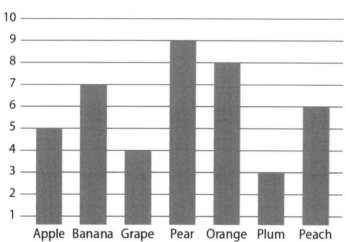

1. Which fruit got the most votes?_____

2. How many more votes did pear get than plum?_____

3. How many more votes did orange get than grape?_____

4. How many less votes did apple get than banana?_____

5. Say true or false: Orange has 3 votes more than peach. _____

6. Say true or false: Plum has 1 vote less than grape. _____

7. Which is the most favorite fruit?_____

8. Which is the least favorite fruit?_____

Draw a Bar Graph

Make a bar graph to show the number of each type of balls given.

prepaze

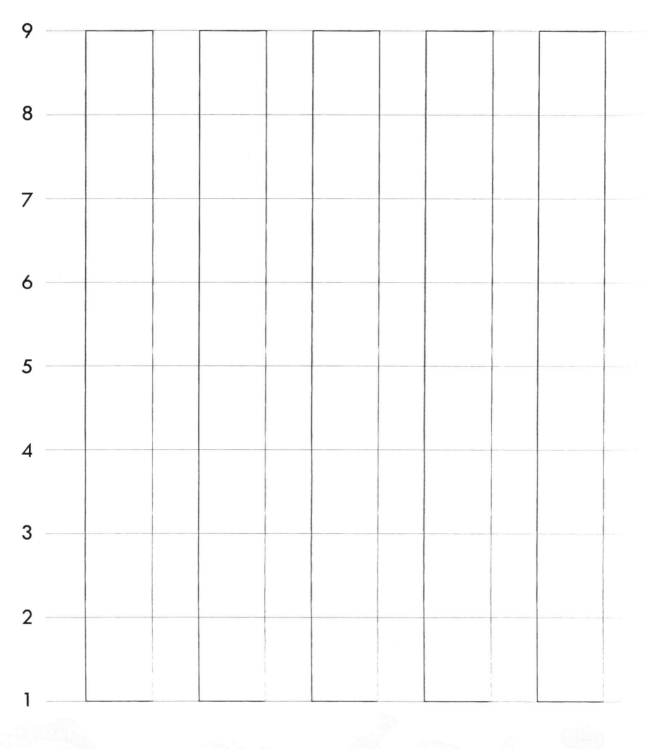

Data Collection and Representation

Answer the following questions and represent your answers on the bar graph.

1. How many students are there in your classroom in school?

2. How many members are there in your family?

3. How many boys are there in your family?

4. How many girls are there in your family?

5. How many days a week do you go to school?

6. How many cars are there in your building?

7. How many friends do you have?

8. How many vowels are there in the english alphabet?

1	2	3	4	5	6	7	8

Fred's farm

The table shows the type and number of animals on Farmer Fred's farm.

Cows	Pigs	Sheep	Chickens	Ducks	Dogs
35	15	25	30	20	5

Use the data in the table and complete the bar graph to show the type and number of animals on Fred's farm.

Remember

1. Label both the axes.

2. Write the scale.

3. Graph the data.

4. Use colors to complete.

Scale: _____

Answers

English Answer Key

Pair It Up!

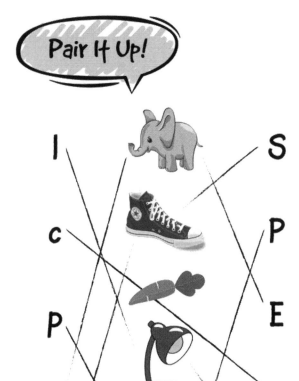

I   S

c   P

P   E

e   C

s   L

Find My Partner

1. s	6. e
2. d	7. r
3. q	8. c
4. k	9. y
5. g	10. h

Spot the odd one

1. D	5. A
2. c	6. e
3. i	7. B
4. X	8. a

Complete Me!

1. FAN	5. PEN
2. MAT	6. SEE
3. BIKE	7. VAN
4. ROSE	8. JAM

prepaze

What Am I?

1. tree

2. rat

3. cap

4. pan

5. dog

6. car

7. fan

8. sun

Complete Me!

1. Erin is <u>Tina's</u> sister.

2. Did you see my <u>cat</u>?

3. This is a <u>children's</u> playground.

4. Lisa and <u>Mike</u> are planting trees.

5. I want a <u>balloon</u>.

Find Me!

Common nouns

1. It is a <u>board</u>.

Explanation: It is a pronoun, and board is a common noun.

2. The <u>basket</u> has <u>oranges</u> and <u>grapes</u>.

Explanation: basket, oranges, and grapes are common nouns.

3. Ana's <u>friend</u> has a <u>garden</u>.

Explanation: Ana's is a possessive noun. Friend and garden are common nouns.

4. This <u>lake</u> is amazing!

Explanation: This is a pronoun, and lake is a common noun.

5. Joe is in the <u>house</u>.

Explanation: Joe is a proper noun, and house is a common noun.

Proper nouns

1. I can read <u>English</u>.

Explanation: I is a pronoun, and English is a proper noun.

2. <u>Pluto</u> is not a planet.

Explanation: Planet is a common noun, and Pluto is a proper noun.

3. His name is <u>John</u>.

Explanation: His is a pronoun, and John is a proper noun.

4. <u>Lisa</u> and <u>Mike</u> watered the trees.

Explanation: "Trees" is a common noun, and Lisa, Mike are proper nouns.

5. <u>Joe</u> is writing.

Explanation: Joe is a proper noun.

Possessive nouns

1. Is this my <u>friend's</u> bike?

Explanation: Bike is a common noun, and friend's is a possessive noun.

2. She is going to her <u>brother's</u> school.

Explanation: School is a common noun, and brother's is a possessive noun.

3. I painted the <u>dog's</u> house.

Explanation: House is a common noun, and dog's is a possessive noun.

4. The <u>wall's</u> color is yellow.

Explanation: Color and yellow are common nouns, and wall's is a possessive noun.

5. It is <u>Lily's</u>.

Explanation: It is a pronoun, Lily's is a possessive noun.

Who Am I?

Miss Jones, chair, book, Sam's bag, window, table, Andy, wall

Sorting Game

Common nouns: doctor, tennis, sun, desk, fish

Explanation: Since these are common names given to every person, thing, or animal, these are common nouns.

Proper nouns: Tom, Jim, Adam

Explanation: The names Tom, Jim, and Adam are specific to these people, and not common to all people. So, they are proper nouns.

Possessive nouns: Ava's dog, Tim's kite, Mia's pen

Explanation: These words show possession of objects.

Color Me

1. common noun
2. possessive noun
3. proper noun
4. common noun
5. proper noun

Secret Word

1. turkey
2. cat
3. bear
4. zebra
5. lion
6. tiger
7. rabbit

What's My Plural?

1. follow
2. wear
3. bark
4. ride
5. plant
6. bring

1. The cat <u>growls</u>.

Explanation: The subject "cat" is singular. Hence, a singular verb "growls."

2. Children <u>hop along the wall</u>.

Explanation: The subject "Children" is plural. Hence, a plural verb "hop."

3. Adam <u>runs fast</u>.

Explanation: The subject "Adam" is singular. Hence, a singular verb "fast."

4. Cows <u>graze in the meadow</u>.

Explanation: The subject "Cows" is plural. Hence, a plural verb "graze."

5. Ships <u>sail in the sea</u>.

Explanation: The subject "Ships" is plural. Hence, a plural verb "sail."

1. The baby sleeps.

Explanation: The subject "baby" is singular, so the singular verb "sleeps" is used.

2. The students learn.

Explanation: The subject "students" is plural, so the plural verb "learn" is used.

3. The teacher reads the book.

Explanation: The subject "teacher" is singular, so the singular verb "reads" is used.

4. Jerry combs his hair every day.

Explanation: The subject "Jerry" is singular, so the singular verb "combs" is used.

5. The girls swim in the pool.

Explanation: The subject "girls" is plural, so the plural verb "swim" is used.

Answers may vary.

1. The boys sing in choir.

Explanation: The subject "boys" is plural, so the plural verb "sing" is used.

2. The dog digs a hole.

Explanation: The subject "dog" is singular, so the singular verb "digs" is used.

3. The girl dances well.

Explanation: The subject "girl" is singular, so the singular verb "dances" is used.

4. Animals are friendly.

Explanation: The subject "animals" is plural, so the plural verb "are" is used.

5. The desk is made of wood.

Explanation: The subject "desk" is singular, so the singular verb "is" is used.

Explanation: sits, looks, draws, lunches, and clicks are singular verbs.

The other verbs eat, open, talk, clean, and jump are plural.

Which one Is Right?

1. The car is on the road.

Explanation: The singular noun "car" needs the singular verb "is."

2. My brothers laugh

Explanation: The plural noun "brothers" needs the plural verb "laugh."

3. Tom lives in this street.

Explanation: The singular noun "Tom" needs the singular verb "lives."

4. They clean the house.

Explanation: The plural pronoun "they" needs the plural verb "clean."

5. My friend visits the doctor

Explanation: The singular nouns "friend" needs the singular verb "visits."

6. The cats run.

Explanation: The plural pronoun "cats" needs the plural verb "run."

Describe Me

Answers may vary.

Word Puzzle

```
            C C X Z N
          O P E B Z A U X
        O L B I K     U Q X
        P W A R W Y       Q Q U
      Z S N M R H K       Z A F
      M Q T F F Y J       B I N T O F C
    H A X N K B V P L Z C G D G J Z N B N U
    L E V O B A K C I C U Y Z S B E F O R E I
  B P F O R Q C A L T Q V F N E A L O N G U K
  W Z F F O K U Q N U X T J X Z P Z S P P
  H D O V O R E D N U Z N E A R C C X R M X C
  V L B T P H V S B E H I N D D I N S I D E Y
  B B Q U J I L X B I F R I W E C N I S C
    V S N Y                   K A V Y
    H E                       O X
```

 **Locate the cat**

 BETWEEN	 ON	 BESIDE
 UNDER	 BEHIND	 IN
 ABOVE	 INFRONT	 NEAR

 **Find Me**

1. They sell toys <u>in</u> their shop.

2. We use umbrellas <u>during</u> rain.

3. She is walking <u>toward</u> the hospital.

4. The worm went <u>behind</u> the vase.

5. I feel something <u>inside</u> my bag.

6. The floor feels cold <u>under</u> my feet.

7. We went <u>with</u> our parents.

8. We can see <u>beyond</u> this river.

 **Complete Me!**

1. The cat is sitting **by** the table.

2. We use umbrella **during** rain.

3. The hyenas are **around** the tree.

4. The animals are **in** the zoo.

5. The mermaid swam **under** the boat.

 **Sentence Writing**

Answers may vary

1. **I** love my mother.

2. **He** is my elder brother.

3. **She** is playing with her friend Susan.

4. Both of **them** are on the same team.

5. **We** both went to a movie.

1. **Someone** took my pencil

2. We can go **anywhere** by train.

3. **Anything** is possible if you try hard.

4. **Many** people like basketball.

5. **Everyone** on the team supports the coach.

1. This is Annie, and this is **her** book.

2. This is my dog, and **its** collar is new.

3. Sam and July called **their** parents.

4. This is my sister, and this is **our** house.

5. David is my friend, and I like **his** cat.

you, my, our, everyone, us.

1. it - its	4. you - yours
2. we - ours	5. I - mine
3. he - his	6. they - theirs

Pair It Up!

Personal noun

1. I played with my football.

2. She had your apples.

3. We have a car.

4. This is her mobile phone.

5. Is this your bag?

Possessive noun

The football I played with was mine.

The apples she had were yours.

The car is ours.

This mobile phone is hers.

Is this bag yours?

prepaze

Sorting Game

Personal pronouns: I, we, he, she, you, them

Possessive pronouns: hers, his, ours, mine, yours.

Indefinite pronouns: someone, anywhere, something, nobody, everyone, each

Describe the Picture

Answers may vary

This or That?

1. Jack **goes** to school regularly.

Explanation: Goes is a present tense verb.

2. Rene **walks** in the park daily.

Explanation: Walks is a present tense verb.

3. Kim **talks** on the phone for long.

Explanation: Talks is a present tense verb.

4. Smith **jumps** on his bed often.

Explanation: Jumps is a present tense verb.

5. Maxim always **lifts** the heavy boxes.

Explanation: Lifts is a present tense verb.

1. My mom **helped** me with my homework last night.

Explanation: Helped is a past tense verb.

2. Oliver **finished** the work an hour ago.

Explanation: Finished is a past tense verb.

3. Nancy **invited** me for dinner.

Explanation: Invited is a past tense verb.

4. Dane **asked** his tutor for help.

Explanation: Asked is a past tense verb.

5. Larry **ate** an apple in the morning.

Explanation: Ate is a past tense verb.

1. They **will arrive** at 12:30pm today.

Explanation: Will indicates future tense.

2. I **will see** you later.

Explanation: Will indicates future tense.

3. Louis **will sleep** early tonight.

Explanation: Will indicates future tense.

4. Julie **will come** tomorrow.

Explanation: Will indicates future tense.

5. Hold on! Grace **will reach** in few minutes.

Explanation: Will indicates future tense.

1. walked   6. knocked

2. jumped   7. boiled

3. played   8. cooked

4. worked   9. talked

5. pushed   10. pulled

1. will eat   6. will do

2. will say   7. will bring

3. will wash   8. will stand

4. will learn   9. will learn

5. will sing   10. will run

1. go   6. cut

2. clean   7. say

3. try   8. fetch

4. ring   9. ride

5. know   10. give

1. happy

2. angry

3. shocked

4. sad

5. sleepy

Spot the Adjectives

good, huge, tall, hard, soft, poor, red, first, and little.

 **Adjectives**

1. scared

2. messy

3. loyal

4. endless

5. worried

 **Describe Me**

Answers may vary

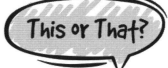 **This or That?**

1. Vance has an **old** bicycle.

2. Mark opened his **new** bag.

3. The **old** fox ran.

4. The bus has **four** wheels.

5. She likes **colorful** leaves.

 **Crossword Puzzle**

Across:

1. but

Explanation: The conjunction "but" is used here to show contradiction.

3. and

Explanation: The conjunction "and" is used to make the subject plural and agree with the plural verb.

4. so

Explanation: The conjunction "so" is used to show result.

Down:

1. because

Explanation: The conjunction "because" is used to show reason.

2. or

Explanation: The conjunction "or" is used as the article "a" is used.

Find Me

1. John <u>and</u> Alfred are captains.

Explanation: The conjunction is "and."

2. You can colour the chilly red <u>or</u> green.

Explanation: The conjunction is "or."

3. I am excited <u>because</u> tomorrow is New Year.

Explanation: The conjunction is "because."

4. David missed it <u>because</u> he came late.

Explanation: The conjunction is "because."

5. Mary is watching Tom <u>and</u> Jerry.

Explanation: The conjunction is "and."

6. Steve likes to pitch, <u>but</u> he does not like to bat.

Explanation: The conjunction is "but."

7. Susie <u>and</u> I have the same dress!

Explanation: The conjunction is "and."

8. The clothes were dirty, <u>so</u> I washed them.

Explanation: The conjunction is "so."

9. Do you want to get your red hat <u>or</u> green hat?

Explanation: The conjunction is "or."

10. I was hungry, <u>so</u> I had an apple juice.

Explanation: The conjunction is "so."

YES or NO

S.No	Sentences	YES	NO
1	My name is Joe.		
2	Ann and Gina are friends.		
3	Excuse me. May I use your phone?		
4	The bus was late because of rain.		
5	My opinion differs from yours.		
6	Wood floats, but iron sinks.		
7	Kelly opened the door.		
8	I can't hear anything because of the noise.		
9	Jeff may or may not win.		
10	Rabbit eats carrots.		

Complete Me!

1. Spiders build web <u>and</u> live in it.

Explanation: The conjunction "and" is needed to show continuation.

2. It's hot, <u>so</u> turn on the AC.

Explanation: The conjunction "so" is needed to show result.

3. Is it a bird <u>or</u> a reptile?

Explanation: The conjunction "or" is needed to show alternatives.

4. Worms eat roots <u>and</u> leaves.

Explanation: The conjunction "and" is used to connect both words.

5. The train stopped <u>because</u> of heavy rain.

Explanation: The conjunction "because" is needed to show reason.

Color Me

1. Steffi **or** Alisa is going to the park.

Explanation: The conjunction "or" is needed to agree with the singular verb "is."

2. Do you play both tennis **and** badminton?

Explanation: The conjunction "and" is used to agree with "both."

3. Camels **and** lizards are found in deserts.

Explanation: The conjunction "and" is used to make the subject plural, for the verb "are" is plural.

4. Is summer hot **or** cold?

Explanation: The conjunction "or" is used to show alternatives.

5. Jacob **and** Jeno are twin brothers.

Explanation: The conjunction "and" is used to make the subject plural, for the verb "are" is plural.

Make Sentences

Answers may vary

Mark It with an X

1. and

Explanation: The conjunction "and" is used to agree with "both."

2. so

Explanation: The conjunction "so" is needed to show result.

3. because

Explanation: The conjunction "because" is needed to show reason.

4. and

Explanation: The conjunction "and" is used to agree with "both."

5. but

Explanation: The conjunction "but" is used here to show contradiction.

Spot the Articles

1. **The** ride is closed.

2. Are you **a** teacher?

3. She has **an** umbrella.

4. Martin travelled around **the** world.

5. Austin is **a** graduate.

6. He is in **the** ranch.

7. Shirley is **a** student.

8. **The** spider has eight legs

9. Ralph is **an** honest man.

10. Frank needs **a** bike.

1. an apple
2. a bird
3. a car
4. a bike
5. an umbrella

6. a banana
7. an orange
8. a student
9. an ink bottle
10. a doctor

```
c  x  p  i  h  n  o  t
k  s  r  e  h  t  n  i
w  a  n  j  m  h  y  b
t  r  l  c  x  i  d  l
h  n  t  h  e  s  e  j
o  v  h  y  q  b  r  z
s  e  c  o  k  c  v  d
e  t  e  s  t  h  a  t
```

This or That?

1. **This** is Julia. (these, this)

2. I know **that** boy. (those, that)

3. I bought **these** fruits for you. (these, that)

4. **That** apple was green. (that, these)

5. Place **these** chairs in line. (this, these)

6. She is good at **that** trick. (those, that)

7. **Those** books are mine. (those, that)

8. **This** is my pen. (this, those)

9. **These** boys are from our baseball team. (these, that)

10. **That** girl goes to my school. (those, that)

Across
2. fish
4. penguin
5. zebra

Down
1. tiger
3. giraffe

Math Answer Key

1.

a. 5 + 5 = 10.

b. 5 + 3 = 8.

c. 1 + 2 = 3.

2.

4 + 10 + 3 = 17. Add all the three numbers. Thus, Angela has 17 items in her bag.

3.

2 + 4 + 6 = 12. Add all the three numbers. Thus, Kevin has 12 trees.

4.

2		8 more boxes have to be colored to make 10
5		5 more boxes have to be colored to make 10
9		1 more box have to be colored to make 10
6		4 more boxes have to be colored to make 10
4		6 more boxes have to be colored to make 10

5.

3 + 2   4 + 1   4 + 9

6.

a. Each duck has 2 legs. 2 + 2 + 2 + 2 + 2 = 10, thus 10 legs in all.

b. Each hand has 5 fingers. 5 + 5 = 10, thus 10 fingers in all.

c. 7 + 4 = 11. There are 11 bees in total.

Garage Sale Problem

7. Any combination of addition sentences that makes the following statements true can be written.

Joe picked 5 toys.

Stella picked 10 toys.

Tom picked 12 toys.

Zach picked 8 toys.

8. Draw five balls in the first box, four balls in the second box and 9 balls in the third box.

9. Use the properties of addition to solve the problem. 5 + 1 = 6 and 4 + 2 = 6

Joel's Marbles

10. Adding 8 balls to 8 balls gives 16 balls. 8 + 8 = 16.

1. 13; 5; 8

2.

48	49	50
		51
		52
		53

3.

$$20 - 9 = 11$$

4. Any two subtraction sentences, where both the numbers are the same. Example: 6 - 6 = 0

Math Bubble

5.

6.

7 - 5 = 4 - 2

7.

a. 17 pens - 2 pens = 15 pens

b. 15 badges - 5 badges = 13 badges

c. 19 dolls - 4 dolls = 15 dolls

d. 16 fans - 3 fans = 13 fans

e. 18 boxes - 5 boxes = 13 boxes

8. The missing number is 3, since 9 - 6 = 3.

1. Using the tens frame,

10 + 4 = 14;

10 + 9 = 19

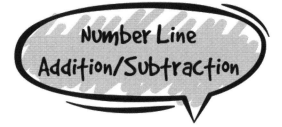

2.　　6
　+　2

Answer: 8

　　　5
　+　1

Answer: 6

　　　8
　-　2

Answer: 6

　　　7
　-　6

Answer: 1

3.

7 + 5 = 12 ; 5 + 4 = 9

prepaze

4.

1	2	3	4	5
6	7	8	9	10

11	12	13	14	15
16	17	18	19	20

21	22	23	24	25

5.

Tens	Ones
2	16

Tens	Ones
5	5

Tens	Ones
4	18

Tens	Ones
3	6

Tens	Ones
4	15

Tens	Ones
5	8

Comparison of Numbers

1.

10	9		8	6

7	1		4	5

0	2		3	10

2.

a. Lydia

b. Monday

3.

a.   <

b.   >

c.   =

4. Answers may vary, a sample answer is given.

4	3		6	4

9	7		1	0

8	6		2	1

All About cakes and Butterflies

1. a.

	Tens	Ones
	3	2

	Tens	Ones
	3	7

2.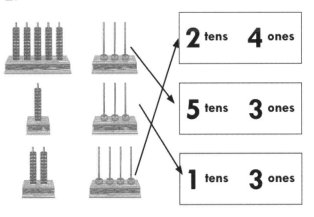

2 tens   **4** ones

5 tens   **3** ones

1 tens   **3** ones

3.

Numeral	Number Name
99	Nineteen
59	Fifty-nine
69	Eighty-nine
89	Ninety-nine
19	Sixty-nine

4.

```
   21              45
  /  \            /  \
 20   1          40   5
```

Bundle Them!

5. a. 54

b. 31

c. 11

d. 39

6.

Join the Dots

7. Students to join the dots in the correct sequence.

Comparison of Numbers

1. a.

8.

a.	**15**	Fifty-one
		Fifteen
		One five
b.	**88**	Eighty-eight
		Eight eight
		Eight
c.	**62**	Twenty-six
		Six two
		Sixty-two

b.

2. a.

b.

2.

a. What is 1 more than 89? 90

b. What is 1 less than 50? 49

c. What is 1 more than 20? 21

d. What is 1 more than 99? 100

e. What is 1 less than 9? 8

f. What is 10 more than 78? 88

g. What is 10 less than 55? 45

h. What is 3 less than 62? 59

i. What is 7 more than 43? 50

j. What is 10 less than 100? 90

Number Bonds

1.

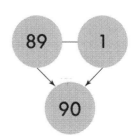

45 — 26
71

89 — 1
90

What Is Jack's Favorite Game?

2.   TENNIS

3.

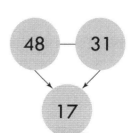

86 — 21
65

48 — 31
17

Read! Draw! Write!

4.

a. 24 + 15 = 39   b. 9 + 18 = 27   c. 17 - 4 = 13   d. 10 + 15 = 25

Number Equation

5. a. 6 + 3 = 9

   b. 7 - 2 = 5

6.

One more than	Number	Fact
9	4	8 + 2
2	10	8 - 1
3	3	9 - 5
6	9	2 + 1
8	7	5 + 4

Color the Pairs

7.

8 - 5	3 + 9
9 + 3	6 + 7
4 + 2 + 7	9 - 6
7 + 8	8 - 2
10 - 4	8 + 7

How Many Squares?

1. a. The pencil is 4 squares long.

   b. The stick is 7 squares long.

2.

Measuring Tool	object
Ruler	Your height
Measuring tape	Pencil
Meter Stick	Book

Arrange

3. a. C A D B

   b. B C D A

Help Zoe Find the Taller Tower

4. Tower <u>Gray</u> is taller than tower <u>White</u> by two blocks.

Tower <u>White</u> is taller than tower <u>Gray</u> by 3 blocks.

Path A or Path B

5. Path A is the shorter path and Path B is the longer path.

Longer or Shorter?

6. a. Red

   b. Pink

   c. Yellow/Orange

   d. Pink and Orange

Circle, Color, or Cross!

7.

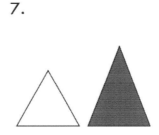

Colour the tallest

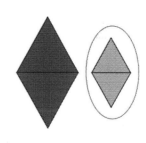

Circle the shortest

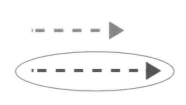

Circle the longest

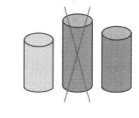

Cross the tallest

8. The answer may vary.

9. The bucket. Because, the bucket is wider and taller than other objects.

10.

11. a.

b.

12. The correct picture is a.

Why? The scale used to measure the triangle in figure b is broken and not continuous.

Help Steve and Rose

13. a. Steve has the shortest piece of cloth. It is shorter than Angela's by 10 - 5 = 5cm.

b. The answer may vary, cause it depends on the child's drawing.

14.

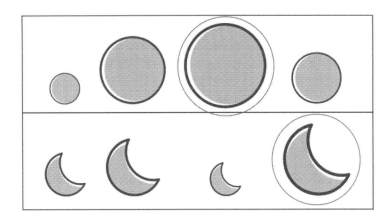

15.

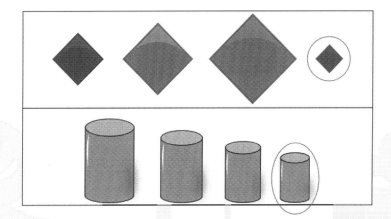

1.

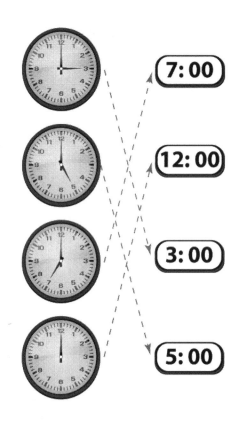

7:00

12:00

3:00

5:00

2.

 9 o'clock

 6 o'clock

 Half past 4

 Half past 11

3. a.  **b.**

4. Playing basketball with friends in the evening - About an hour

Drawing and coloring cartoon - About an hour

Pouring water in a glass - About a minute

Tying a shoelace - About a minute

calendar Problem

5. a. 28 days

   b. Tuesday

   c. 25th

6. a.   b.   c.

7. Hour hand is between 8 and 9 Minute hand is at 6

   Time is 8:30

   _____

   Hour hand is between 5 and 6 Minute hand is at 6

   Time is 5:30

   _____

   Hour hand is between 9 and 10 Minute hand is at 6

   Time is 9:30

   _____

   Hour hand is between 2 and 3 Minute hand is at 6

   Time is 2:30

9.

8.

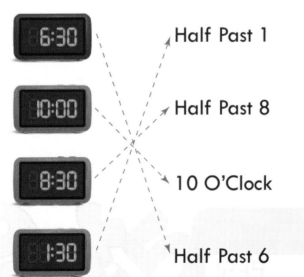

Half Past 1

Half Past 8

10 O'Clock

Half Past 6

Which is the favorite fruit of Ms.Rosy's class?

1.

a. 10

a. Mango

b. 1

c. 23

2.

a. 3 more

b. 2 more

c. Green and purple

d. Red, Pink, Green, Purple

Dominoes

4.

a. 9 dots

b. 3

c. 3 more

d. 8

World of Sea Animals

3.

Which Movie to Watch?

5.

a. Ice age

b. Spiderman

c. 18

d. 2

James Vegetable Garden

6.

a. 3

b. 7

c. 4

d. 17

7.

a. Hamster

b. Rabbit

c. 9

d. 2 more

8.
a. 7
b. Basketball
c. 18
d. 5
e. No

9.
a. 2 days
b. 2 days
c. 1 day
d. More rainy days

10.
a. None
b. John and Olivia
c. 9
d. Eva

11.
a. Toy truck
b. 6
c. 2 more
d. 8

12.

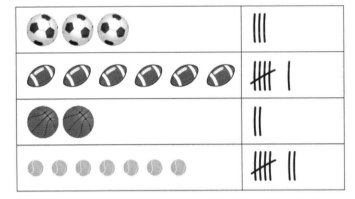

Corners and Sides

1.

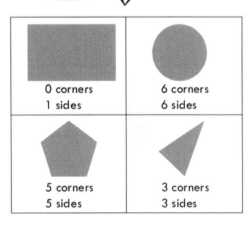

13.

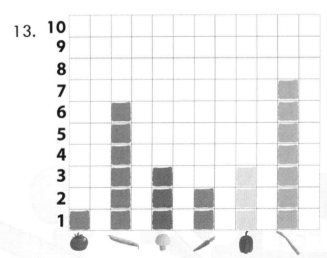

Circle Them Up!

2. a.
b.
c.

3. A square has 4 sides of equal length. Thus, is not a square.

4.

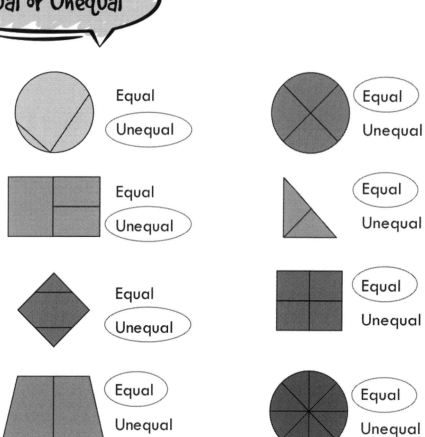

Equal   (Unequal)

(Equal)   Unequal

Equal   (Unequal)

(Equal)   Unequal

Equal   (Unequal)

(Equal)   Unequal

(Equal)   Unequal

(Equal)   Unequal

5. When two square are joined a rectangle is formed.

6.

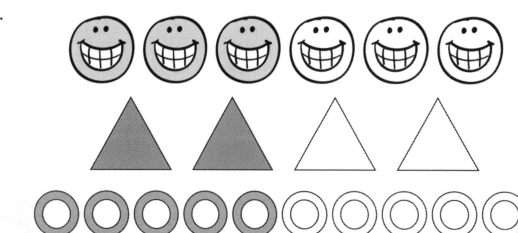

7.

Alison	Eva	Sasha

8. Answers may vary.

9.
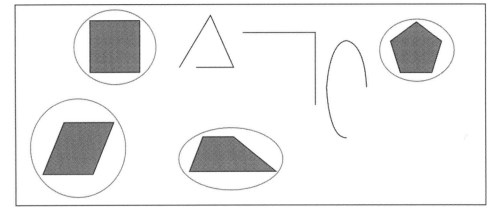

10.
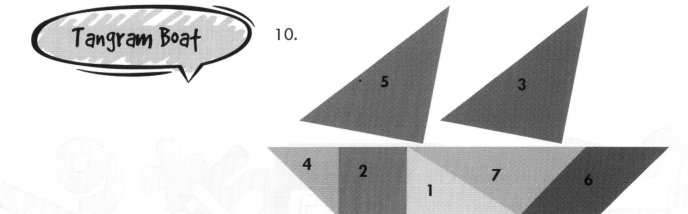

11.

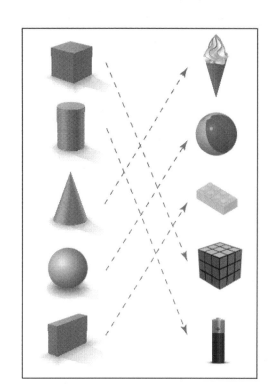

12.

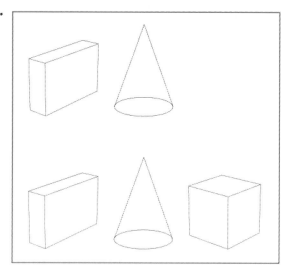

13.

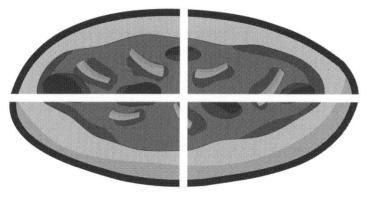

14.

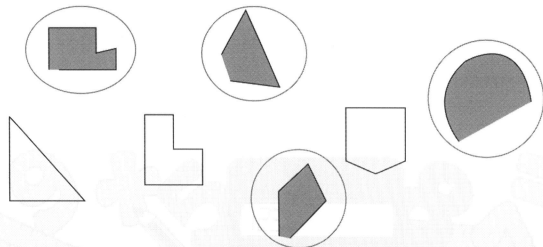

15. Triangle - 4 Rhombus - 2

16.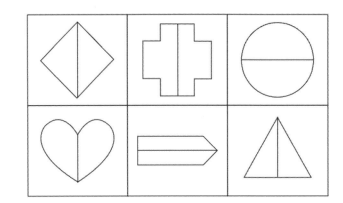

Pattern

17.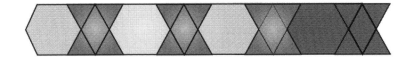

18. No. The cube will fall if it is placed on top of a cone.

19. 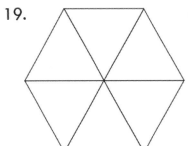   6 triangles.

20.

Share and care!

21.

Steve	Marcus	Joe

22.

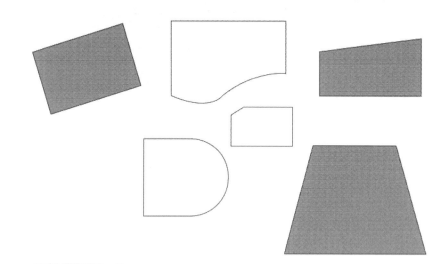

 Riddle Time!

23.

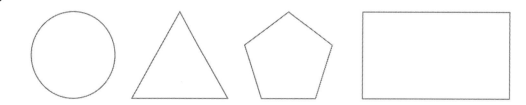

24.

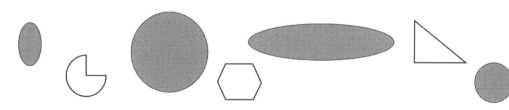

25. It has 5 sides. It is a closed shape. It has 5 corners. **26.**

a. The shapes have 3 sides. The shapes have 3 corners

b.

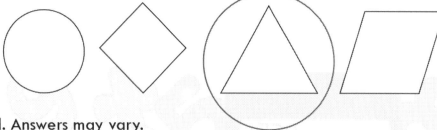

c. & d. Answers may vary.

27.

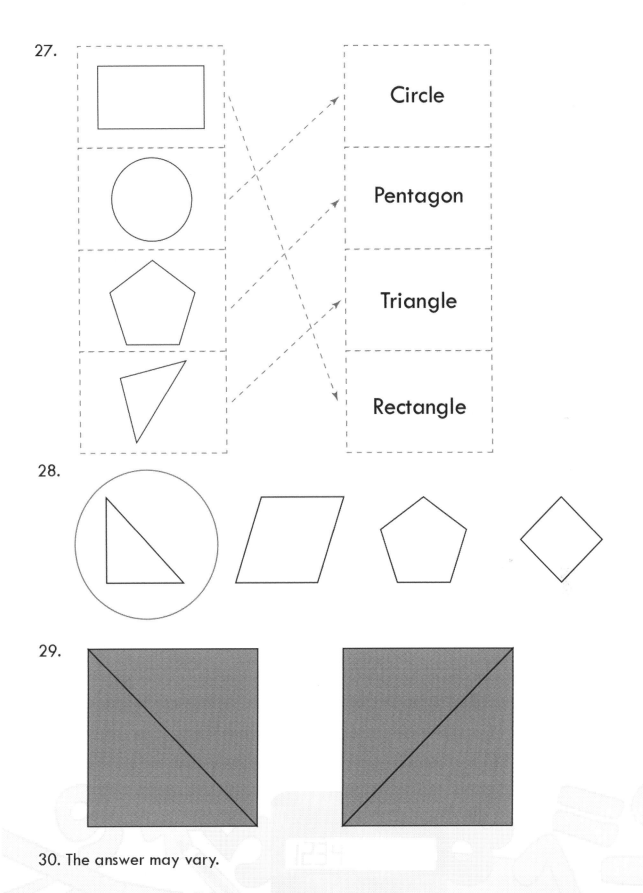

28.

29.

30. The answer may vary.

1.

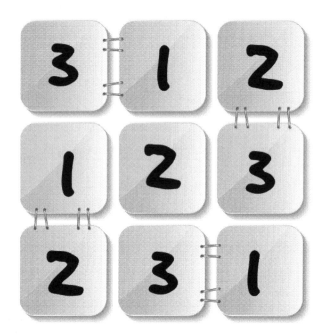

2.

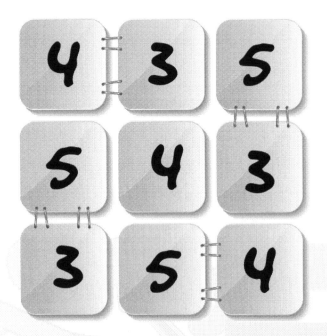

Science Answer Key

Solid, Liquid, or Gas

- Gas, because it expands to fill space

- Solid, because it is hard

- Liquid, because it flows

- Liquid, because it flows

- Solid, because it has a fixed shape

- Gas, because it expands to fill space

Forms of Matter

Light gray - liquid

Black - solid

White - gases

exhaust	juice	orange	steam
soda	milk	brick	oxygen
pencil	helium	table	wood
rain	snow	smoke	ketchup

True or False

1. False, living things are also called matter.

2. True

3. False, solids have a fixed shape.

4. True

5. False, liquids take the shape of the container they are in.

6. True

7. True

8. False, there are 3 states of matter.

9. True

10. True

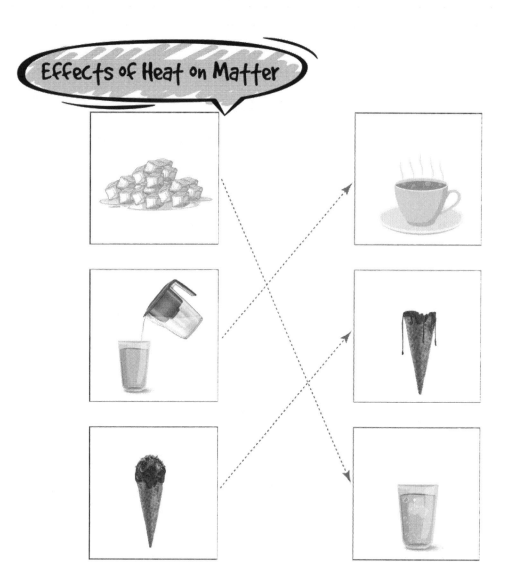

1. Ice melts when heated

2. Water evaporates on heating

3. Ice cream melts when heated

Process of change in States

1. Heating   4. Mixing

2. Cooling   5. Cooling

3. Heating

Word Grid

F	A	H	M	T	G	P	U	J
R	J	V	S	C	U	D	K	M
E	V	A	P	O	R	A	T	E
E	G	N	V	O	P	M	B	L
Z	B	O	I	L	A	S	I	T
E	I	W	A	N	G	C	A	D

Water and Heat

1. Vapor, evaporation, because heat is added to water

2. Ice, freezing, because heat is removed from the water, that is the water is cooled here

3. Water, melting, heat is added to snow

Water cycle

1. Vapor, evaporation

2. Vapor, condensation

3. Tiny droplets, large droplets fall as rain

4. Water from plants, vapor

Parts of a Plant

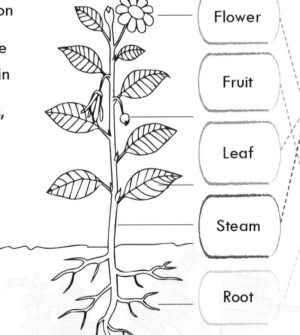

Flower — Holds the plant upright

Fruit — Usually green and prepares the food for the plant

Leaf — Absorbs water and nutrients from the soil

Steam — Helps the plants to produce seeds that grow into new plants

Root — Many are good to eat and they protect the seeds

1. Kind of animals, crocodile, crocodile is a reptile while other animals are mammals

2. Food, fox, fox eats meat while other animals eat plants

3. Body covering, crow, the body of crow is covered with feathers while the other animals are reptiles with scales on their bodies

4. Habitat/place of living, frog, here frog lives on land while other animals live in the sea

5. Body covering, dog, the body of dog is covered in hair/fur while the other animals are birds with feathers on their bodies

6. Habitat/place of living, monkey, monkey lives on trees while the other animals live on grasslands

Eating Habits of Animals

Eats Plants	Eats Animals	Eats both Plants and Animals
cow	tiger	cat
sheep	lion	dog
panda	wolf	crow
bee		bear
elephant		ant
giraffe		human

1. Snake, reptile, scales, trees, small animals
2. Horse, mammal, hair/fur, grassland, grass/plants
3. Eagle, bird, feathers, trees/forest, worm/small animals
4. Clown fish, fish, scales, sea, worms/plants
5. Lion, mammal, hair/fur, forest/grassland, other animals
6. Lady bug, insect, shell, grassland/forest, smaller insects

Food Chain

1. 1,4,2,3
2. 3,1,4,2
3. 3,4,2,1

What's the weather like?

Sunny, cloudy, windy, snowy, rainy, stormy

Identify the Instruments

1. Thermometer - used to measure temperature
2. Rain gauge - used to measure rainfall in an area
3. Wind vane - indicates the direction of wind

Reading Thermometers

1. 70, 0, 90, -10, 30
2.

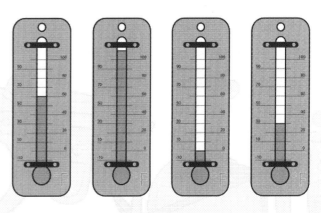

1. Pear

2. 6

3. 4

4. 2

5. False

6. True

7. Pear

8. Plum

Draw a Bar Graph

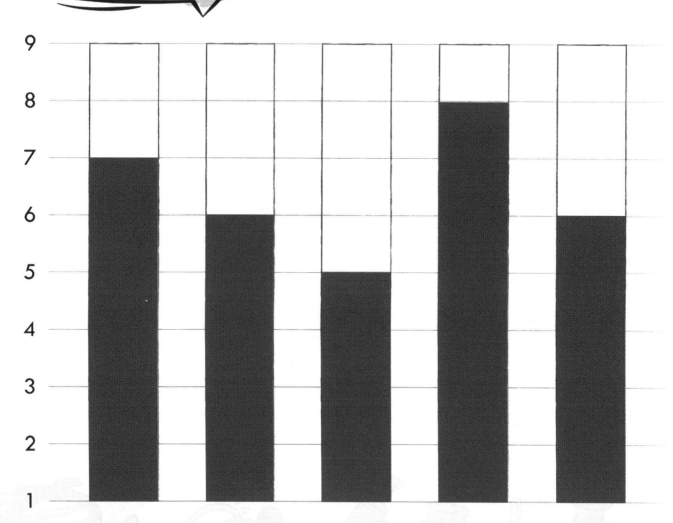

Number of Animals

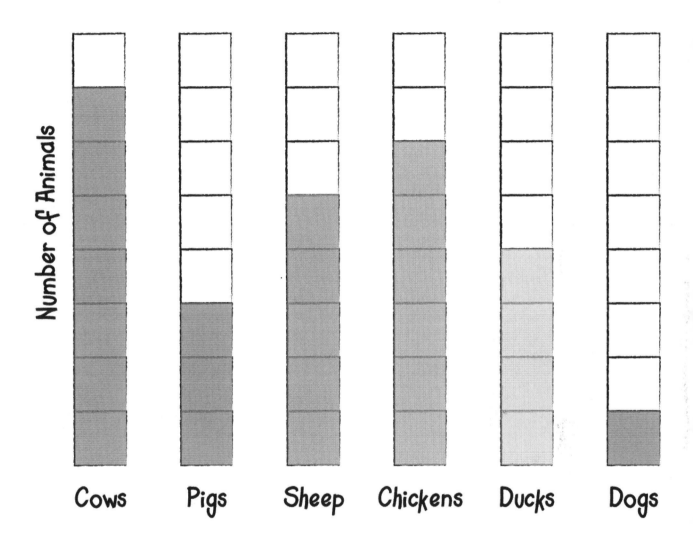

Cows   Pigs   Sheep   Chickens   Ducks   Dogs

Scale: 1 unit = 5 animals

prepaze

www.aceacademicpublishing.com

THE ONE BIG BOOK

GRADE 1

For English, Math, and Science

Ace Academic Publishing

ACHIEVING EXCELLENCE TOGETHER

Made in the USA
Columbia, SC
06 August 2021

43099197R00141